Initiations and Interactions:

Early Intervention Techniques for Parents of Children with Autism Spectrum Disorders

Teresa A. Cardon, M.A., CCC-SLP

APC

Autism Asperger Publishing Co.
P.O. Box 23173
Shawnee Mission, Kansas 66283-0173
www.asperger.net

8-09

85852093

© 2007 Autism Asperger Publishing Co.
P.O. Box 23173
Shawnee Mission, Kansas 66283-0173
www.asperger.net

Publisher's Cataloging-in-Publication

Cardon, Teresa A.
 Initiations and interactions : early intervention techniques for parents
of children with autism spectrum disorders / Teresa A. Cardon. –
Shawnee Mission, Kan.: Autism Asperger Pub. Co., 2007.

  p. ; cm.

  ISBN-13: 978-1-931282-32-1
  ISBN-10: 1-931282-32-3
  LCCN: 2006934649
  Includes bibliographical references.

  1. Austistic children–Language. 2. Asperger's syndrome–Patients–Language.
  3. Autistic children–Behavior modification. 4. Autism in children. 5. Communication
  disorders in children. I. Title.

RJ506.A9 C37 2007   2006934649
618.92/85882–dc22   0611

Printed with Avenir and BlackJack.

Printed in the United States of America.

Dedication

I must first dedicate this book to my incredible family. They are the reasons that I do what I do. Thanks to Craig for the continuing support and encouragement. I am who I am because you knew I could be. And thanks to Rylee and Breelyn for the parenting lessons you have taught me, and continue to teach me, especially the ones that I take a long time to learn.

Thanks to Mom, Tiffany and Michelle for always being willing to listen, even when my overzealous ideas don't make sense. Thanks for answering the middle-of-the-night phone calls.

Thanks Dad for never being shocked when I take on "one more thing." Your confidence in me always gives me that extra boost.

Thank you, Grandma Joy, for being so proud.

Thanks to everyone at AAPC who makes this look like a work of art and brings it all together so perfectly. You are an amazing team, and I am proud to be the humble recipient of all your knowledge and talent.

Last, but definitely not least, THANK YOU to all of the amazing families that I have been privileged to work with over the years. Many of the ideas and strategies in this book came about from the phenomenal work that I see you do with your children. Thank you for sharing your children with me. This book is for them.

– Teresa A. Cardon

Contents

Introduction

How long should I play with my son?" a mother asked in a parent training session, truly wanting a concrete answer. Seeing my somewhat contemplative look, she rephrased the question. "I mean, do I need to play with him every hour for half hour or for twenty minutes of every hour – how long should I play with my son?"

I have heard the phrase "every moment is a teachable moment" numerous times, and while I am a firm believer in the concept, I have to ask – every moment? As a mother of two young daughters, I can testify that the laundry, the cooking, the errands, and the day-to-day paperwork of life also need to get done. So although every moment COULD be a teaching moment, in the real world every moment CANNOT be a teaching moment.

I have thought long and hard about the question "How long should I play with my son?" and the earnestness with which it was proposed. It is in an effort to answer it that I set out to write this book. What truly is a parent's role in early intervention? In a world of sometimes multiple "therapies" prescribed for children with autism spectrum disorders (ASD), how parents fit into the equation can be a bit confusing.

I have run across many families for whom the adage of "Mom's Taxi" (sorry Dads, that's how the saying goes!) is an accurate description. Many parents of children with ASD have a full-time job taking their children to multiple therapies, and the time they don't spend in the car going from social skills training to OT is often booked at home waiting for the next therapist to arrive. Then there are the children who remain on waiting lists for months at a time receiving no services at all. And finally, there are families who live in areas where certain therapies aren't even available.

How do parents find a balance and, most important, what is right for their child? Research suggests that intervention should begin early in order to minimize the severity of the developmental delay or disorder as well as the behavioral, social and family disruptions that have been found to be related to ASD (Wetherby & Prizant, 1993). Early intervention – not waiting on a list for six months, nine months, twelve months – NOW! In fact, more and more autism experts are trying to help physicians become more aware of the characteristics of ASD (e.g., Autistic Disorders Screening Kit, Melmed, 2003; First Signs Screening Kit, 2001) to ensure that they address this early intervention component. The earlier the intervention begins, the better! Although there is some controversy over "best practice" therapies in the world of autism, I think all the experts would agree – early is best! But that takes us to a central problem – availability of therapists!

Parents as Partners

I would like to propose a shift in thinking when it comes to providing "therapy" for children on the autism spectrum. Not only has research indicated that "early" is key, research has also shown that for early intervention programs to be successful, they must involve a child's primary caregivers. A family-centered system recognizes that the family is the center of the child's life and the "absolute constant" (Koegel & Koegel, 2006). In fact, parents' responsiveness has been related to an accelerated rate of language development in typical and high-risk children alike (Rocissano & Yatchmink, 1983). If families remain dependent upon the often unavailable services of specialists, they are not only depriving their child of whatever help they can provide right now, they are also depriving themselves of the sense of empowerment that accompanies taking responsibility for helping their child.

Many parents are eager and able to assume the role of primary intervention agents for their children. Because parents have more frequent and extensive contact with their children than do clinicians and are generally more motivated to persist (Tannock, Girolametto, & Siegel, 1992), they are able to effect more change in their children's development. Parents can also provide intervention at more frequent intervals during the day, over a longer period of time and under conditions that may be highly motivating for the child. By creating the ideal learning environment, we can prime children for language learning and developmental growth at an optimal pace (Girolametto, 1988). To create an ideal learning environment, parents must learn specific teaching strategies that have been found to be highly effective when working with children with ASD.

I must take a moment to clarify my position here. I am not advocating the removal of all therapies and specialists from your child's weekly regimen. I am attempting to put more control into your hands. I have watched too many families "wait" while precious time is lost – unsure of where to begin to help their child. So if your child is currently seeing several therapists, take the tools you find helpful in this book and make sure that a "family-centered" approach is part of your weekly regimen. If your child is one of the thousands who have been "wait-listed," wait no more – the tools are at your fingertips!

I would also like to take a moment to emphasize that while I am advocating a "family-centered" approach, I am not insensitive to the intense demands that a having a child with ASD places on the family. Parents are concerned with "their child's level of dependency, difficulty managing problem behaviors, cognitive impairment, limits on family opportunity, and life-span care" (Koegel & Koegel, 1995, p. 81). The stress of dealing with these concerns – not to mention the financial burden and the strain that is placed on the husband-wife relationship – can be overwhelming.

It is understandable, then, that some parents feel incredible stress when told that they must now also provide crucial early intervention to aid in their child's development. Do what you can. Seek support from family members, friends, doctors, support groups, psychologists, educators. It is a long road, and not one to be traveled alone.

It is important for families and professionals alike to realize that parents can decrease family distress and improve the quality of life for the entire family when they work directly with their children (Gallagher, 1983). Strategies that employ more naturalistic teaching methods have been shown to reduce depressive symptoms and result in happier parent-child interactions and a more positive communication style (Bristol, 1993; Koegel & Koegel, 2006). There is also evidence that parents who attend trainings and receive education in treatment strategies experience reduced overall stress, decreased frustration and increased self-confidence and ability to handle problems involving their child (Baker, Landen, & Kashima, 1989).

This guidebook offers parents a training tool as they set about navigating the unknown and often overwhelming world of ASD. The ideas and strategies discussed are not some new "therapy" to be added to an already busy schedule. My goal is to put effective techniques into a simple format that parents and caregivers can remember and utilize every day in every way!

We have been focusing on parents and how they can create better initiations and interactions with their children. I do not mean to exclude professionals. In fact, I hope that many professionals will find this book helpful as well. However, parents must be a key component in early intervention. Therefore, it is important that professionals view parents as partners in intervention. It doesn't matter what professionals do in therapy for one hour a week unless there is carryover at home. Parents need to know exactly what is going on in the therapy room. So, invite them in! Have parents join you in practicing the strategies you are working on. Have children practice their skills with you and their parents foster generalization of skills. Parents need to feel empowered to engage with their children, so be their guide.

I am not insensitive to the fact that some parents believe their child does better when they are not in the room. I understand parents want their children to be able to make the most of their time in therapy. If a child does better when her parents aren't in the room, it is even more imperative that you bring the parents into the room to give them the tools they need to engage successfully with their child.

There is an old saying, "It takes a village to raise a child." When it comes to raising a child with ASD that sentiment couldn't be more true. We all must work and plan as a team together to help a child be successful. Everyone must have the child's best interests at heart. It is my hope and dream that a child's happiness and success be the driving force behind any interventions and supports that are put in place.

CHAPTER 1

Initiators vs. Responders

When I ask parents, "How does your child let you know when he is hungry?," one of the most common responses I get is, "I have to kind of guess." This brings me to a key concept that I want to address in this book. In order for a child to let a parent know that he is hungry, he needs to be able to initiate some sort of action toward the parent. The ability to *initiate* is vital to the overall success of a child. Not surprisingly, initiation is often described as a "pivotal" behavior. That is, children who can initiate are able to get others to respond to them and, in turn, improve their communication and language skills (Koegel & Koegel, 1995).

Children with ASD are often great little "responders" but they are not often great initiators! Being great responders means they figure out pretty quickly that when someone says something, they are expected to *do* something. Whether they produce a sign, point, say a word, create a sentence or find a picture, they know it means they need to do something.

In fact, because children get so good at realizing that some type of response is required of them, it is not uncommon to see them go through a whole repertoire of responses, hoping to hit on the key one that will finally get them a desired result. I call it the baseball coach syndrome. Children sign "more," "eat," or "help" all within a matter of seconds over and over and over again, trying to get a highly desired object – looking very much like the third-base coach telling a runner to head for home. In this case, the children are not even aware of the meaning of the signs they are producing. They are just "responding" to the verbal output and the really motivating item that is being held just inches from their grasp.

Setting up Opportunities to Initiate

Children who are unable to initiate in order to get their needs and wants met in the home environment are most certainly unable to initiate to get their needs met at school, in the community and later as grownups in the workplace – I think you get where I am going with this! *It is imperative that we teach our children to initiate at an early age.*

As a parent, one of my many jobs is to help my children. I help them get breakfast in the morning, tie their shoes, do their homework … and the list goes on and on. In fact, sometimes I help them with things they haven't even asked for help with. As parents we can often predict what our children may need. After all, when they first wake up in the morning, it is a pretty safe assumption that breakfast time is not too far off.

But what happens when we become too good at predicting what our children need? Is it possible that instead of helping, we are actually hindering?

As a speech language pathologist one of the things I say over and over again to parents and families is "Avoid anticipating your child's needs!" Sounds easy enough, but turning off those natural "helper" instincts can be difficult. But in order to encourage a child to initiate, we need to do just that! We

need to give a child a reason to come to us and initiate an interaction. When we use our parental powers of prediction, we may actually be discouraging their initiation skills.

Take breakfast, for example. Does a child have any reason to come to me and "ask" for juice when I already have the juice cup on the table and ready to go? What if, instead of having juice in a cup, ready to go, you place the bottle of juice on the counter where the child can see it but can't reach it? It may not seem like much of a difference, but in order to get what she wants, your child has to intentionally send a message by reaching for the juice, pulling you to the juice or asking for the juice. The opportunity to initiate would have been lost if the juice was already in a cup on the table.

If we want our children to become great initiators instead of just great responders, we have to set up situations that require our involvement.

In other words we need to increase our child's dependency on us. Sounds crazy, I know – aren't we supposed to be encouraging our children's independence? YES, eventually, but not just yet! Be forewarned, when you avoid anticipating your child's needs, you will make life more difficult for yourself – at least initially. Isn't it just more time efficient to have the morning juice ready to go? Of course, it may seem easier, and there are moments when life gets hectic and we just don't have time to set situations like this up, but in the long run too much "help" does hinder a child's long-term independence. To become an effective initiator – and eventually an effective communicator – your child must realize the power her actions and words can have. It is imperative, then, that we give children as many opportunities to initiate as possible.

Remember, independent initiations occur without a request, "What do you want?" or a reminder such as, "Say, 'I want juice'."

Teaching How to Initiate

Now that you know how important it is to set up scenarios where your child has opportunities to initiate, we need to talk about HOW you're going to *teach* your child to initiate. If you leave the juice sitting on the counter where your child can see it but not reach it, you need to think about what your child will do next. If the first thing that comes to mind is "throwing a mad, angry tantrum on the floor because he really wants his juice in a cup," you need to be very clear (and quick) about how you are going to *teach your child HOW to take his turn* to initiate. It may be as simple as physically helping him grab your hand and pull you to the juice.

Be sure you have a clear idea in your head so that you are not caught off guard in the moment. Sometimes it is helpful to write down your expectations: "I expect my child to pull me by the hand to the juice to ask for juice." Writing it down is also helpful because everyone in your child's life will know exactly what your child's turn in the interaction is.

In the SCERTS model (Prizant, 2002), Barry Prizant reports that children do well when events have

- clear beginnings
- a sequence of logical steps
- a sense of completion

For example, when you play Ring-Around-the-Rosie with a child, begin by stating the name of the game and holding out your hands. When the child takes your hands, you start to sing and spin in a circle. When the song ends, you "all fall down." You then ask, "Again?," and start the sequence over again. When you are going to play the game for the last time, you state, "One more time." When you have finished playing the game for the last time, you clearly state, "All done" and make an all-done gesture with your hands. Every time you play Ring-Around-the-Rosie you follow the same sequence.

PECS. One of the most effective tools I have came across to teach a child with limited or preverbal skills to initiate is the Picture Exchange Communication System (PECS) (Frost & Bondy, 2002). PECS is a systematic program that teaches children how to use pictures to get their needs and wants met. One of the things I value about PECS is that initiation is built right into the stages of the program. So in our previous juice scenario, if your child wanted the juice, you would teach him to give you a picture of juice to request "juice."

Each stage of PECS is important for overall success, and I encourage you to find a trained specialist to help you get started if you are not familiar with the program. A trained specialist will have taken a two-day training course offered by Pyramid Educational Consultants and should have certification to verify the training. PECS will be discussed in more detail in Chapter 7.

Adequate time. This brings me to another point. In order to determine if your child is capable of initiating for juice on his own, be sure to give him adequate time to initiate. Many experts in the field of autism (e.g., Koegel & LaZebnik, 2004; Prizant, 2002; Quill, 1996; Sussman, 1999) encourage an extended wait time so that a child has an opportunity to process the auditory information going in, problem solve, plan a response in his head and then create the motoric planning required to verbalize or execute an appropriate action.

The average length of time that I see parents and professionals wait for a response from a child is often less than three seconds. When I suggest that you give your child adequate time to initiate, what I mean is WAIT – really WAIT!!!! I recommend waiting for 15-30 seconds so that your child has time to process the auditory information, determine a response and then implement the motor planning process required to respond.

> *Using pictures is NOT the same as the Picture Exchange Communication System. Too often parents tell me that the child's school and therapists are using the PECS (or "pics" as I often hear it referred to) system when, in fact, they are using visual supports, not a true Picture Exchange Communication System. Be aware that there is a great difference. You can find specialists trained in the PECS program to work with your child or you can be trained yourself in the PECS program.*

Some parents have told me that waiting 15-30 seconds for their child to initiate would be impossible because the child would lose interest and move on to something else, and then any chance for an interaction would be lost. To solve that problem I use a strategy I like to refer to as *Watch & Wait*.

When you *Watch & Wait*, you take cues from your child. You watch to see if your child appears to be trying to communicate. Watch for signs that she really wants to get the highly motivating item that is before her. It may be that the child is not sure HOW to get the item she is interested in. If that is the case, then your job is to teach her how to initiate her turn.

Here and in the following, initiating is equated with turn taking.

When you *Watch & Wait* you will learn when your child is unsure of how to initiate (take) her turn. You can then guide her to success with the appropriate turn-taking cues, including

- physical cues
- verbal prompts
- verbal commands
- partial modeling
- commenting
- "raised-eyebrow wait"

Physical cues. There are many different techniques we can use to cue children when they are unsure of how to take their turn. One of the most basic cues that we can use to ensure a child is successful is to *physically*, hand-over-hand, help him take his turn. That may mean shaping his finger into a point and helping the child point to the item he wants. It may mean physically helping his hands form a sign such as the sign for "more" or "cookie" to ask for what he wants. Or, as with PECS, it may mean physically helping the child exchange a picture to get what he wants.

Verbal prompts. Another way to cue a child to successfully take her turn is to *verbally* prompt. Several types of verbal prompts can be used to assist a child. If a child's language skills are emerging but she tends to borrow or echo other people's words, you can verbally provide the exact words she can use to initiate for what she wants. Fern Sussman (1999) refers to this type of prompting as "interpreting" for your child. It is a helpful way to think about cueing a child who is very echolalic.

For example, if a child loves bubbles and reaches for the bubbles to indicate that she wants to play with them, you can simply interpret her reaches by saying "bubbles." A child who echoes will likely say "bubbles" immediately following your production. Even for children who are not verbally responding, the *interpret* strategy is very helpful to supply children with the labels they will ideally begin to echo. As her verbal language skills increase, you can change the way you interpret by adding another word, to make a more complete request, "Want bubbles."

I want to be sure to clarify something here: When children first begin to communicate verbally, they typically begin with one-word utterances. (Yes, there are children who begin talking in full sentences, but that is another story altogether!) To be more precise, children usually start to communicate with *one-word labels*: juice, ball, bubble, car, milk, and so on. When children discover that their words have the power to motivate and bring another human being into action, they begin to unlock one of the mysteries of two-way communication. Their words induce quick and accurate responses and their verbalizations become very reinforcing, motivating them to produce them again and again. Also remember that one word can have multiple meanings. For example, the word "ball" can mean "I want the ball," "Where is the ball?" "I see the ball," and so on. Why then are we so determined to rush right past this stage and move to two-, three- and even four-word sentences?

Children progress through stages of language development. If a child's development is delayed, the stages of language development are also delayed. When children first learn to communicate verbally, they are so excited that someone finally understands what they want. They have a new sense of control over their lives. Imagine how frustrating it would be to have the bar raised right away – before they are ready to move into the next developmental stage of language.

> *Although great at ensuring success, physical prompts or cues are very intrusive and require the most adult involvement. Physical prompts can even be detrimental if a child becomes dependent on them. Therefore, they should only be used in the initial phases of teaching a child the turn that is expected of him.*
>
> *Physical prompts should be faded, or gradually reduced, as soon as possible so that a child does not become dependent on them.*

Immediate Echolalia: Exact repetition of words produced immediately after the original production. Example: Adult: "Do you want some milk?" Child: "Want some milk."
Functional Purposes: (a) to indicate an affirmation or "yes" response; (b) to label objects, action or location (Prizant, 2005).

One-word requests stay around for quite some time. I can't tell you exactly how long, since each child is very different, but don't be surprised if your child requests things using one word for a long time. A guideline I like to follow is this: A child should have a pretty good handle on fifty or so words (Koegel, 2004) and be able to spontaneously initiate using those words before being expected to combine multiple words.

If a child is expected to use two-, three- and even four-word sentences before he is ready, communication breaks down. Communication breakdowns often lead to what people refer to as "behaviors." I think of "behaviors" as a child's way of expressing frustration and anger. After all, isn't that what a "behavior" really is? Imagine the following scenario.

A child who initiates for a drink by saying "juice" is all of a sudden required to repeat the sentence "I want juice, please" in order to receive her favorite sippy cup filled with her very favorite drink. Not surprisingly, the child may get very "impatient" (substitute "angry" and "frustrated") at suddenly having her requests ignored. Impatient and frustrated children tend not to be effective communicators.

It may sound ridiculous to hear a speech language pathologist warning against utterances. After all, aren't I supposed to be the one helping children increase their language skills and expand their utterances? True, but I want to propose that we wait just a bit longer before we start insisting on increased sentence length – again think about the fifty-word guideline! That is not to say that we stop modeling the appropriate way to ask for something. When a child states "juice," I am thrilled to hear a parent say, "I want juice." An appropriate and consistent model goes a long way. Think about all the things you have heard your child echo in the past whether you intended it or not. When we appropriately model longer utterances for our children, they will eventually echo our sentences, too.

Verbal command. As a child's language skills increase, another way we can verbally cue a child is to provide a verbal command. Verbal commands typically come in the form of "Say _____." I often see verbal commands used too quickly and intrusively. When adults provide verbal commands on a constant basis, the *Watch & Wait* strategy goes right out the window.

Verbal commands used too often and without appropriate wait time contribute in a big way to the "responder" problem discussed earlier. I have found verbal commands to be more successful after I have used the "interpret" strategy for quite some time. Moving straight to verbal commands usually ends up with a child repeating the entire command. For example, an adult might state, "Say hello" and a child will repeat, "Say hello." If you find that verbal commands aren't effective, back up and use the *interpret* strategy. The *interpret* strategy has less room for error and taps into a strength many children already possess.

Partial modeling. Another type of cueing I have found to be very helpful is referred to as a partial model. Sometimes children just need us to jumpstart their motor planning and initiating by giving them a piece of a word or a part of a sentence. For example, if a child wants juice and sees it sitting on the counter, use the *Watch & Wait* strategy to determine if he can ask for it independently. If you determine that he is struggling with knowing how to take his turn and ask for the juice, simply say the first sound of the word, "juuuuuuuuu." This small prompt can help to get things started without you actually directing the whole exchange. The prompt is minimally intrusive and gives the child a hint, which is often sufficient to get him on the way to successful communication.

Commenting. Another favorite cueing strategy is simply to make a comment directed at what the child is interested in. When I put something highly motivating in a big clear plastic jar that a child cannot open on his own (Wetherby & Prizant, 1989), a whoopee cushion, for example, I often just comment by saying something like, "That whoopee cushion looks like fun!" or "I want to play with that!" Then I direct my attention the entire time to the jar on the table. Similarly, if I know a child loves a certain type of food, I may take a bite and comment on how yummy it tastes. This enticement usually encourages the child to reach for the food, label the food to indicate a request or state, "I want some," to get her needs met.

As mentioned earlier, when you use the *Watch & Wait* strategy, you can discover what the child is interested in and then make a comment directed toward the item, "I like cars!" I like this strategy for several reasons: It is not as intrusive as many of the other strategies discussed and comments are something we want children to learn how to use eventually anyway.

"Raised-eyebrow wait." I can't talk about cueing without including the ever-popular *"raised-eyebrow wait"* as it has come to be known around my clinic. It seems to be a pretty universal facial expression that we make when we are trying to indicate that another person is supposed to take his or her turn. You know the one I mean, mouth open, eyebrows raised, eyes wide open looking very expectant. Since this expression is so universally used, it is probably the most natural thing we can due to prompt a child to take his turn. Of course, it is not always enough of a prompt and that is why the *Watch & Wait* strategy and the previous prompts are so important. But as children learn how to take their turns and become less dependent on us for cues, the raised-eyebrow wait can be a very effective tool.

Initiation is a pivotal skill that children with ASD will need to be taught directly as part of early intervention. Research has identified a child's ability to initiate as a good indicator of more favorable long-term outcomes (Koegel & Koegel, 2006). By using the strategies discussed in this chapter, you will give your child more opportunities to initiate in an often fun and natural way that doesn't require major investments of time, materials and other resources.

CHAPTER 2

Communication Environments

I mentioned before that it is imperative that we give children as many opportunities to initiate as possible. Now that I have presented you with some theory behind that claim and some cueing strategies to help your child learn how to take her turn, let's get down to the nitty-gritty and map out exactly what we can do to create opportunities for children to initiate.

I urge families to create a COMMUNICATION ENVIRONMENT! We create opportunities for a child to initiate and communicate by creating environments that encourage communication. Let's break this down room by room.

In the Kitchen ...

Creating an organized and structured system in the kitchen goes a long way toward increasing a child's desire to initiate and interact. The kitchen is usually a central place where families gather and opportunities to communicate are plentiful. Besides, it is where food is prepared and often eaten, and food is typically (although not always) a great motivator.

The following suggestions are simply that – suggestions. The key is to organize your living space so it works for your family and increases your child's opportunities to communicate.

Be sure that you keep favorite snacks on hand because when a child is taught to bring a picture in exchange for a favorite snack, you want to be able to reward his initiations and communication. NOTE: With all the talk about childhood obesity these days, please keep your child's health and proper weight in mind when dispensing snacks. There are lots of healthy snack options.

- **Snack Bins**

Containers with favorite snacks should be clear so that a child can see what is inside. Take a picture of the snack inside and velcro it to the front of the container. You can also use copies of the photograph for visual schedules, choice boards and picture exchange systems. (See examples of these visual supports in Chapter 7.)

Snack bins should be difficult for the child to open so that he cannot get the snack out himself. Remember, we are setting up the environment to encourage communication right now – not independence. If your snack bins are in a cupboard or pantry, you can place a choice board (see Chapter 7) on the front of the cupboard or pantry showing the snacks that are available.

- **Cabinet Locks**

Now you may be thinking, "No bin is too difficult for my child to open." That is where another strategy comes into play. If you haven't been using them already, it may be necessary to install cabinet and door locks in areas where you keep food and other highly desired items. Sometimes it is difficult to find child locks that are truly child proof for a particular child. Many children with ASD get very good at meeting their own needs without communicating in a more traditional way, including beating the world's best child-proof systems. Be aware that children will problem solve on their own to get what they want, even if it means climbing to the top of the refrigerator!

Be sure that when you place highly desired items out of reach or under lock and key extra precautions are in place to ensure that the child's safety is maintained. Many of the families I work with have gone through a variety of child locks, but eventually they find one that works in their household. The idea here is that highly motivating snacks and food items must be tucked away so that your child has to communicate to get her needs met.

- **Height Can Be Your Friend**

  Placing high-interest items just out of reach also sets up opportunities for a child to initiate. She can see what she wants but she cannot get to it without your help. This is not recommended for children who are agile, fearless climbers. Remember, we need to teach the child HOW to ask for what she wants – be it pulling a parent by the hand or verbalizing. Children get frustrated if they do not understand what we expect them to do to get what they want, which can escalate into behavioral outbursts and even meltdowns.

- **Make It Visual!**

  I mentioned using snack pictures to create visual supports in the kitchen. Beyond that, a number of visual supports can help to create a communication environment in the kitchen. Choice boards on the refrigerator are a great option. Often daily schedules and weekly schedules are present in the kitchen as well, as it is typically a central gathering point for the entire family.

  Another great way to create visual supports in the kitchen is to use a personal placemat for the child. A foam placemat with pictures or drawings to represent where the spoon, fork, plate and cup should go can help a child ask for the items needed. If you place a fork and cup on the placemat and conveniently forget the plate, the visual reminder of the plate encourages the child to initiate communication to get the plate. (Again don't forget to teach HOW to ask for the plate several times and then *Watch & Wait* to see if the child can initiate for the plate on her own.)

  Some children do better with picture cards that use magnets as opposed to velcro. Velcro can become highly stimulating for some children, making them so fixated on the velcro that the picture loses all meaning.

  There are many different ways to display visual supports. Should they be vertical or horizontal? Should I use photographs, line drawings or words? Can my child understand a schedule with more than two or three things represented? These questions and many more will be addressed in the Chapter 7, *Visual Supports Every Day in Every Way*.

- **A Jarful of FUN!**

    During snack time, placing a favorite snack in a see-through jar (again, one that is difficult to open) on the table is another great way to encourage children to initiate. They can see the snack and will try to get the jar open, but when they are unable to do so, you will be on hand waiting for them to initiate that they need help.

    It may take several tries and multiple cues before your child begins to initiate, but remember *you have to teach him HOW to take his turn*. How is he supposed to "ask" for help: placing the jar in your hands, placing your hand on top of the jar, signing "help," verbally requesting "open," etc.? Your job is to be consistent and persistent. Expect the same response every time. If it doesn't happen and you have waited an adequate length of time, go to your prompts.

In the Family Room ...

A family room (or another room in the house where the family tends to congregate if no formal family room is present) is meant to be just that – a room where the family can gather. Too often, however, family rooms become cluttered, overstimulating parking lots for miscellaneous "stuff." For a child with ASD this is not a communicatively friendly environment.

Be sure that walls are not too busy with lots of things hanging, that paint colors are not overwhelming (one child whom I worked with couldn't stand the color red) and that a clear physical structure that defines the space for specific activities has been established. If not, you run the risk that the child will be distracted and unable to function.

- **DVDs**

  Favorite show selections can be highly motivating. If your child is a master at working the electronics in your home and can easily get a show on without any help from you, it is time to create some communication opportunities. This usually means relocating the DVDs to bins or shelves where they are out of immediate reach.

  Many families find that children will climb bookshelves and entertainment centers if they think there is the slightest possibility they can reach a DVD on their own. In a world of 52-inch screens, this can be a dangerous. It may be a better option to place discs in a separate room or closet and provide the DVD cases for your child to use as requesting tools. You can also take pictures and create a choice board and then help your child learn to initiate a turn.

- **Electronics**

  If you don't mind your child working the electronics in your house, relocating the electronics is, of course, optional. But think of the initiations you can create by placing the DVD player out of reach. You can create another opportunity for initiation by standing with your finger hovering above the play button just waiting for the sign (word, picture card, etc.) to push "start." Getting a DVD to play is usually a highly motivating activity.

  Think about the opportunities the computer offers. For example, using a choice board with pictures of all the computer games instead of allowing the child direct access to the games is another way to set up the environment to encourage communication. Use the *Watch & Wait* strategy while you hold the computer mouse hovering over the correct icon. If your child needs a prompt, you can model the word "play" as you click on the icon.

- **Toys**

  A couple of key points are important when it comes to toys in the family room. *First, toys need to be contained and organized!* Too often there are toys EVERYWHERE. While I recognize that cleaning up after your child is a daunting and difficult task, a little planning and organization goes a long way. Those clear bins with tight lids that I recommend for snacks work well with toys, too. Since you will be buying some for the kitchen anyway, why not grab some extras to use for toys?

  I have found it helpful to take pictures of what is in the bin and then velcro the pictures to the end of the bin. Even though I usually use clear bins, it still is helpful to provide a visual, especially if you will be using the same photograph on a choice board or picture exchange system. Limit the number of bins your child has access to at one time, or the scenario of toys everywhere will quickly return.

  Once a child has indicated the toy she is interested in playing with, whether through reaching, picture exchange, choice boards or verbalizing, I often wait before I open the bin to give the child another reason to initiate. The children I work with get pretty quick at initiating for "open" because I am consistent every time we get something new out to play with.

  Shelves and cabinets that limit access to toys is another great communication environment strategy. One family I worked with organized cabinets by the types of toys they contained. One cabinet contained all "pretend play" toys, one cabinet had games, another construction toys, and so on. And then each individual bin in the cabinets was clearly identified with a photograph, and cabinets were labeled "PRETEND PLAY," "GAMES," "CONSTRUCTION TOYS," etc. This is just one more way to make a little organization go a long way.

- **Make It Visual!**

  I have already suggested how to make individual areas of the family room more effective with visual supports such as choice boards, bins, labels, and so on. Other visual supports can be incorporated in the family room as well.

Many children on the autism spectrum have difficulties with transitions, making it difficult for them to have to turn off the television or the computer and go to another activity. Visual supports to aid in transitions can be extremely helpful. For example, use a timer to visually indicate how much time is left to watch a favorite show. Using a "Stop Light" system is another way to prepare a child for a transition. When the clip is on green, it is time for the activity to continue. When the clip moves to yellow, it is just about time to stop, and when the clip finally moves to red, the activity is over. Timers and stop lights let a child know when it is time to end an activity as opposed to the adult deciding the activity is over and, therefore, help prevent arguments.

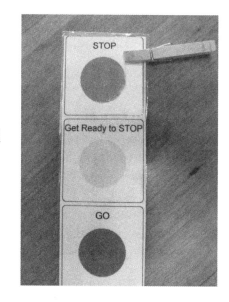

Another idea along those same lines is to place five pictures of the computer or television on a velcro strip where the child can see it. The final picture on the strip is that of a stop sign. At various intervals (maybe five minutes, maybe one minute, depending on what your child responds to best), you can remove a picture from the strip. When the final picture comes down, the "stop sign" indicates that the activity is finished.

- **Physical Structure**

    The Treatment and Education of Autistic and related Communication Handicapped Children (TEACCH) model (Eckenrode, Fennell, & Hearsey, 2005) emphasizes the importance of clear physical structures in classroom settings to encourage success. A clear physical structure makes it evident what activity is to happen in a given space and helps a child know what to focus on. A good physical structure also helps to minimize distractions in the environment.

    Creating a clear physical structure in the home environment is important. For example,

I see families using book shelves and desks to create an organized space for the computer station, using couches and chairs to create physical boundaries in an often overwhelming space in front of the television. I have even seen families use tape on the floor to give their child a visual sense of structure in a room. A child can end up with an overwhelmed sensory system when receiving too much input. A clear visual structure helps a child with ASD determine what details are relevant.

- **Cozy Corner**

  A family room is often a place where families go to relax. Creating an inviting space for your child with bean bag chairs, large pillows, cozy blankets, etc., can be a way to help her find some comfort for often overwhelmed sensory systems. I once worked with one family who hung a swing from the ceiling (be aware of space and safety issues on this one!) to help their daughter find comfort in the family room.

In the Bathroom …

It seems that children either love bathroom routines or hate them. If your child loves bath time, this is a great way to create opportunities to initiate. If your child is not a fan of bath time, be sure to focus on first establishing a positive environment and then go on to create a communication environment.

To create a positive environment, think about bringing favorite toys into the tub, sing some favorite (and distracting) songs while the child is in the tub, give the child cups to pour with, and so on. If your child does not like getting water on his face, give him a washcloth to cover his face with or have him put on a sun visor when you rinse his hair out. Sometimes giving your child something to chew on (toothbrush, oral motor support) can help him remain more self-regulated in the tub. The key is to create a positive association with the routines in the bathroom.

- **Make It Visual!**

  You can provide visual supports in the bathtub to help your child recognize what the routines look like. If your child is not very fond of bath time or teeth brushing, create a "first/then" board (see Chapter 7) to help her "see" what the reward is that will occur immediately after the bath or teeth brushing.

  Some people have negative perceptions of rewards, but if you think about it, we all set "rewards" for ourselves in our heads – "If I just finish this last report, then I can get up and take my coffee break!" Or "If I save a little each week, we can take that trip to Florida." So what is wrong with rewards, so long as it is not the only strategy used with your child?

  It is also important to put up a self-help schedule that you and your child can refer to during a routine. Think about including self-help schedules for teeth brushing, bath time and pottying. One mom found that her child would sit happily on the potty when she was watching a DVD of children also sitting on the potty (several DVDs are available in this area. I happen to like "Once Upon a Potty").

- **Physical Structure**

  It is possible to provide a clear, physical structure even in a space as small as a typical bathroom. For example, provide your child with a teeth-brushing sequence basket. Divide the basket into sections, and then place a toothbrush in the first section, toothpaste in the second section and in the final section a cup for rinsing. Similarly, in a medicine cabinet or drawer, visually identify where objects are to be placed. Helping your child get organized is key to increasing independence with self-help tasks.

In the Bedroom ...

Too often when I walk into a child's bedroom, I am instantly overwhelmed with the large amount of toys scattered throughout the room. Many children become disregulated, unable to maintain a calm and focused state when too much visual input is presented at one time. Take a look at your child's bedroom to see if it is visually overstimulating.

- **Physical Structure**

  You can create a physical structure in the bedroom just like you can in any other part of the house. Bookshelves and toy shelves can provide physical boundaries if the space is otherwise too overwhelming. Rugs on the floor to indicate boundaries have also proven to be effective with many children. One family I work with uses a rug and bean bags to create a cozy corner in one corner of the room. They use a "transportation" rug in the toy area of the room and have a "train" rug under the train table.

- **Toys**

  The same concept that we applied to toys in the family room applies to toys in the bedroom. Clear, lidded, well-marked bins to hold toys not only help keep the room organized but also provide children with a reason to initiate, provided you are using bins that your child cannot open on her own. Remember: The goal is to have the child initiate for "help" opening the bin.

  *Remember your prompts here – you need to **teach your child how to initiate** asking for help. For example, you may want your child to place your hand on the bin to request for it to be opened. You may want your child to sign "open." Or you may expect the child to exchange a picture to get the container open.*

  Regardless of what communication system you use, be sure your child has a clear understanding of what he is expected to do. Then keep the structure of the routine going by expecting him to ask for help each and every time he wants to get into a toy bin.

- **Make It Visual!**

  Visual supports are just as essential in the bedroom as they are everywhere else in the house. Visual steps to the bedtime routine can be a handy tool if your child struggles with bedtime (pajamas, book, kisses, lights-out, sleep). It is also helpful to label where things go in the bedroom. It is never too early to help your child begin understanding the importance of organizational thinking. Organizational thinking is a skill that will become imperative to success later on in school and is often a challenge for individuals on the autism spectrum.

  You can place pictures of the toys on the toys shelves – the bin with the same toys inside gets placed on the shelf with the matching picture – now we are working on our matching skills too. You can also use pictures to label drawers to help your child identify the contents of the drawer.

This is obviously not an exhaustive list of suggestions. In fact, I learn great new tricks and ideas from families that I work with every week. It is the concept behind these suggestions that I really want to get across. *We need to stop anticipating children's needs in order to encourage them to communicate! Then we need to teach them how to take their turn so that they can learn to communicate!*

A Few More Ideas

If you feel like I am adding fifty new things to your already busy to-do list, there are plenty of other ways that you can encourage your child to initiate. The following communication strategies can be incorporated into your lives by just creatively tweaking the activities that you are already involved in on a daily basis. Let's take breakfast, for example.

- *Be the keeper* (Sussman, 1999) by offering pieces of a banana instead of the whole banana. Your child then has to initiate to ask for "more" banana.

- Play *hide-n-seek* with a cereal spoon in a coffee can. The spoon in the can makes a great noise (beware of sensory sensitivities), and you can tempt the child by peeking into the can on occasion and making a comment about what you see.

- Have a *jarful of fun!* (Wetherby & Prizant, 1989) by putting favorite foods in a clear jar with a tight lid. Then teach your child how to ask for help getting the jar open.

- Offer *parts not wholes*. Place the juice on the table but leave the cup on the counter, then make a big deal about what's missing. "Hmmm, I wonder what I need?" or "I need a cup, where is it?" The key is to make it fun so that the child is coaxed, not forced, into the interaction. You can then see what prompts your child needs to learn to take his turn to initiate to get the cup.

> One other thing I want to emphasize is that every environment that your child participates in should be a communication environment. This means if your child spends part of her day at Grandma's, then Grandma's house needs to be set up with the same types of supports that your child has at home – clear bins with toys, visual supports, and so on. If your child is at a babysitter's, day care or preschool, again, the environment must encourage communication just as the environment at home does. Remember, your child needs the consistency and the structure to make even more progress.

- *Make a mistake on purpose* (Greenspan & Wieder, 1998). Try buttering toast with a fork. Being silly gives your child a chance to initiate to correct your mistake.

Think of these five strategies as the communication tools that will help build more opportunities for your child to communicate. Also, creating communication environments not only gives your child more opportunities to communicate, they provide your child with multiple opportunities to initiate. And initiation is a key to the overall success and development of your child regardless of the activity she is involved in.

CHAPTER 3

Focus on the Interaction, NOT the Activity!

O ver the years I have taught communication training classes to thousands of parents. During these trainings, certain strategies and techniques tend to rise to the top as the most effective or the most important. When working with families impacted by ASD, I always emphasize: Focus on the interaction, NOT the activity! In fact, parents who attend my sessions probably hear me use that phrase so often that they can recite it in their sleep (which is fine with me because it means I am getting my point across). But what exactly does it mean?

When I say, "Focus on the interaction," I mean look at *everything* but the activity! Is your child aware that you are part of the activity? Is your child interested in you being there? Is your child sharing enjoyment with you during the activity? Is your child emotionally regulated and content during the activity? Is your child able to gaze at you to determine if you are interested in the activity? Is your child able to draw attention to herself for social engagement during the activity? Is your child able to make requests to further the social enjoyment going on during the activity?

How are we going to turn everyday activities into interactions? If your child enjoys spinning blocks, opening and closing doors, wandering in circles, or other activities that are seen as "autistic" or "stimmy," remember that these activities can be turned into effective interactions!!!

These self-stimulatory activities often meet a sensory need. Children on the autism spectrum are often over- or underreactive to sensory stimuli. Children take in information from the world through their senses. If this input is not processed correctly "learning to pay attention, learning to engage with others, and learning to communicate may all be affected" (Greenspan & Wieder, 1998, p. 37). It is essential, then, that we find a way to create interactions around children's sensory needs to help them process and regulate their sensory input.

Turning Sensory Activities into Interactions

Let's think about the sensory needs a child may have and how we can turn sensory activities into interactions.

Visual input. If your child seeks out visual input because she is undersensitive to visual stimuli, you might see her lining things up, spinning objects, flicking objects back and forth, viewing objects with peripheral vision, and so on. These activities all provide visual input, but how can we possibly include ourselves to turn them into interactions?

Let's take the activity of lining things up. You can use the *keeper* strategy and hold onto the objects that your child is adding to the line. This sets up a reason for her to interact and communicate with you because she wants to continue adding pieces to the line.

You could also *make a mistake on purpose* and "pretend" to add something silly to the line that doesn't belong. For example, if your child is lining up trains, put an airplane or a dump truck in the line-up. If your child pushes your addition away, you can interpret for him and say "no truck." You are teaching the child to protest in an appropriate manner, and you are giving him a very motivating reason to communicate.

If your child likes to spin objects, invest in tops that she really enjoys but cannot spin on her own. I have seen some very talented parents who can spin blocks, Legos, pegs, or whatever else they discover their child is motivated by. Try a pinwheel. It provides tons of visual input and most children (and even some grown-ups, for that matter) have a difficult time blowing on them just right in order to get a good spin going.

Physical input. If your child tends to seek out physical input because he is under-sensitive to the signals he receives from his body, you are in a bit of luck because it is difficult to find tactile and pressured input without the help of another person. Imagine trying to squish yourself with a pillow. Clearly, it is not as effective as having someone help you.

Your child may try to seek out this type of input by climbing under pillows or crawling into tight spaces, but he can quickly learn that it is more effective to enlist the help of a grown-up. Keep a soft blanket around to create a kid burrito and wrap the child up inside a couple of times and then teach him how you expect him to ask for more; for example, by exchanging a picture of a blanket to ask for more, signing for "more," saying "blanket" or even lying back down on top of the blanket to request the burrito game again. These aren't things children can do alone, so teach them to come to you once they figure out what a great support you are.

What if your child seeks out sensory input by spinning around in circles, how can you possibly turn that activity into an interaction? This is a tricky one. I encourage parents to join in the spinning. On numerous occasions parents have reported back that although they felt unsure and silly at first, their child truly saw them in a different way as they got involved in the spinning and, in the end, the spinning activity turned into a giggling, fun, reciprocal interaction.

> You can find great stretchy blankets that feel almost like a cocoon when you are wrapped inside.

Movement. Many children on the spectrum are constantly on the go. These are the children I refer to as the movers and shakers. They are not quite sure where their body needs to be or what they should be doing, so they just keep moving and shaking until it feels right. There are many fun activities you can turn into interactions if your child is constantly seeking out movement.

A swing in the backyard can be very motivating, and if you pause mid swing, you give your

child a reason to communicate with you.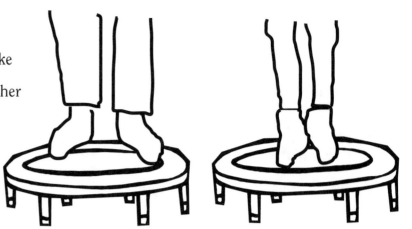
Again, be sure to teach the child how to take
turns so she does not get frustrated. Whether
it is verbally requesting more, exchanging
a picture card for "more," signing for
"more," or just wiggling and connecting
with a fleeting eye glance to request
more, you are turning an activity into an
interaction.

If your child loves trampolines, think of all the games you can play bouncing together. You can bounce fast and slow, high or low, you can even *make a mistake on purpose* and forget how to bounce or fall down and laugh until you are both feeling silly. Include yourself in the moment and watch what interactions come about!

We cannot take away a child's need for sensory input. Think about all of the "self-stimulatory" things that grown-ups do: nail nibbling, pencil tapping, pen clicking, pencil chewing, leg bouncing, humming … the list goes on and on. As many smokers will attest, the minute they quit smoking, they seem to gain twenty pounds. The desire to have something in their mouth is a sensory-based need. Once the cigarettes are gone, they replace the sensory input of cigarettes with food.

Your child's sensory needs are real. Instead of fighting a losing battle to extinguish them, try to replace them with more appropriate or socially acceptable behaviors – and while you're at it, turn some motivating activities into communication interactions.

CHAPTER 4

Music Mania

Music has been found to be an effective tool when helping children learn to communicate as certain neurological components of music and speech originate in the same area of the brain and travel similar pathways (Michel & Jones, 1991). Since that is the case, I say sing everything!

If your child responds to music and seeks out auditory input, find ways to include auditory input throughout the day. Music is a tool that can easily be incorporated into daily activities and routines. Music also provides natural ways for your child to take a turn and participate in an interaction. This chapter provides some easy-to-use musical tools that you can add to your daily interactions with your child.

Movement

In Chapter 3, I mentioned that many children seek out movement to meet their sensory needs. A great way to turn a movement activity into an interaction is to add a song. While you are jumping on the trampoline, for example, you can sing about jumping – "Johnny's wearing his jumping shoes, jumping shoes, jumping shoes. Johnny's wearing his jumping shoes all day long." After you have sung the song numerous times, you can stop jumping and wait for the child to fill in the blank before you start again. Or you can pause and wait for the child to initiate jumping again before you continue to sing.

Many parents have found success when they use songs with movement activities built right in. As a child, my parents sang a pony-riding song with me while they bounced me on their knees. Sign up for a "parent and me," also known as a "mommy and me," type singing class (these and similar programs are offered inexpensively through city recreation programs) or buy a DVD that can teach you lots of songs and movement activities. You will be able to create great interactions and add communication opportunities after your child has learned the routine and gets excited about asking for more and more.

Daily Activities

You can also sing about daily activities your child is already involved in, such as "This is the way we brush our teeth, brush our teeth, brush our teeth. This is the way we brush our teeth so early in the morning." Singing about daily routines helps a child to learn the steps of the routine and increases receptive understanding of what is happening during the routine. It also encourages the child to learn self-help skills. Sing songs during dressing routines, pottying, clean-up time, and so on, to increase your child's familiarity with the skill.

Again, it is important to think about the communication environment. Sing the same song every time your child brushes her teeth and print the song out and post it in the bathroom so everyone can sing it with your child. Send a copy to school and to Grandma's house so that all of your child's transactional supports can include the teethbrushing song. The same goes for the dressing song, the potty song and the clean-up song. *Repetition and consistency are key when working on receptive and expressive communication skills.*

Many children learn better when they are given an opportunity to learn through different modalities. When you include music in routines, your child not only has an opportunity to practice the routine in the same way every day, thereby increasing cognitive and muscle memory of the sequence, he also hears the routine through song every day. The more learning modalities you tap into, the more capable your child becomes of learning the activity.

Introducing New Cognitive Concepts

You can introduce new learning concepts through song: "What does a cow say? Moo, Moo, Moo!" "What color is an apple? Red, Red, Red." The alphabet, animal names, colors, shapes, and so much more, can be learned through music. Think about popular children songs. Many of them already have cognitive concepts built in. For example, the song "Head, Shoulders, Knees and Toes" teaches children the names and locations of body parts. "One, Two Buckle My Shoe" introduces numbers and counting. "Five Little Monkey's" teaches another concept with numbers, counting backwards.

You can also get creative with familiar songs by making slight changes to teach new skills. "Baa, Baa Black Sheep" can be expanded to include "Baa, Baa blue sheep, orange sheep, red sheep . . .," and so on. Don't forget to include colorful pictures of sheep as you sing to help reinforce the color concepts. You can help your child learn names of family members, friends and others when you make slight changes to the "Brown Bear Brown Bear" story line. Simply change the words to fit your child's name and then add in the names (and, of course, include the pictures) of the people you want your child to recognize. The song then goes something like this, "Johnny, Johnny who do you see? I see Mommy looking at me. Mommy, Mommy who do you see? I see Grandpa looking at me . . .," and so on, and so on. The possibilities really are endless. And don't forget – music should always be lots of fun.

Introducing Language Concepts

As a speech therapist I often work on language concepts through music. To work on the concepts of "he" and "she" with a child I was seeing, we created the song "When we talk about a girl, we say SHE. When we talk about a girl, we say SHE. When we talk about a girl, when we talk about a girl, when we talk about a girl we say SHE!" (tune of "If You're Happy and You Know It …").

A fun way to work on prepositions is to use the song "On top of old smoky." I change the words to meet the child's needs, so it might turn out something like this: "*On* top of the table the tiger will sit" or "*Under* the chair the tiger will hide" or "*Next* to the farm house the horse will rest." The idea is to use music to teach the prepositions the child is working on.

After we have worked on the song together for a while, I add in the child's turn. I place the animal next to the farmhouse and *Watch & Wait* with a very expectant "raised eye-brow" look on my face while I give the child a chance to take a turn and fill in the preposition. If need be, I resort to prompts to help the child be successful. I always think about the goals I have for the child and the turn that I expect him to take, in this case expressing the appropriate preposition. The turns set up during the interaction must be very clear.

Sequencing Skills

I also work on sequencing skills through music. Some of my favorite songs are "There Was an Old Lady Who Swallowed a Fly," "Slippery Fish" and "The Wheels on the Bus." I always provide something visual, typically a flannel board story, so the child not only hears the sequence as we sing it but also sees it visually.

The first turn I typically encourage a child to take is simply to take the flannel piece from my hand and place it on the board. Next, I pause before I name the flannel piece, giving the child a chance to name it. Then I hold up two different pieces and ask the child to label and choose the correct piece for the sequence. And finally, after the child is really good at filling in the blanks and knowing the sequence, I *make mistakes on purpose* (handing the child the wrong piece or holding up two of the wrong pieces to choose from) so that he can correct me and demonstrate good understanding of the sequence. Remember we have to teach a child *how to take a turn* and we also have to teach him *where to take the turn*. Music gives us many opportunities to do just that.

Introducing New Skills

You can also introduce and teach new skills using a song. Waiting in line for a turn on the swings was difficult for one of my kiddos, so we created the song, "Stand and count. Stand and count. Wait my turn. Wait my turn. Then I get to swing, then I get to swing. Stand and count. Wait my turn" (tune of "Frere Jacques").

Another little guy was learning to play ball with his mom, so we created the song "Roll, Roll, Roll the ball, Roll the ball to me, Roll Roll Roll the ball, Roll the ball to me." (If you haven't already guessed, the ball song was created to "Row, Row, Row Your Boat.")

Be sure to write down the words of songs when you create them as well as the tune. This is helpful for a couple of reasons: (a) you don't forget the words or the tune; and (b) everyone else involved in your child's day can sing along, too.   Another suggestion – keep it simple! We want the child to be able to learn from the songs, so limit the words and focus on the key concepts you want to get across. By the way, this not only helps the child learn the song, it helps all the grown-ups learn the songs and stick with them, too!

If you feel overwhelmed at the thought of having to make up songs, you might want to go on the Internet and search for songs. Many talented people are more than happy to share their ideas, and I have found many songs by typing in a few key words in a search engine. I also have used search engines to find great visual supports to go along with songs.

I type in key words for a favorite song, the "Itsy, Bitsy Spider" or "Brown Bear, Brown Bear," for example, and then glance through some websites until I find what I want. I am always amazed at the great visual supports that I can find. Many parents and teachers have made it very simple to create visual supports for some of the most popular children's songs and stories by posting them on the web.

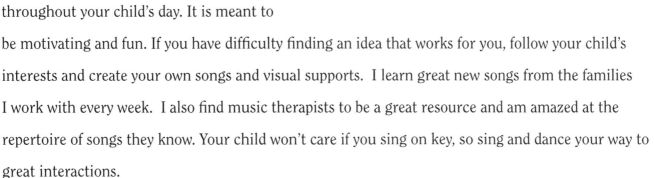

To make the visual supports last longer, I print them on cardstock and laminate them. This is also a quick way to make flannel board stories. Once you have the pictures printed up and laminated, all you have to do is add a "hook" piece of velcro to the back and they will stick to any flannel board.

Music is a tool that you can use throughout your child's day. It is meant to be motivating and fun. If you have difficulty finding an idea that works for you, follow your child's interests and create your own songs and visual supports. I learn great new songs from the families I work with every week. I also find music therapists to be a great resource and am amazed at the repertoire of songs they know. Your child won't care if you sing on key, so sing and dance your way to great interactions.

CHAPTER 5

Turning Books and Story Time into Interaction Time

When families initially come to see me as a speech and language pathologist, I ask how their children respond to books and story time. Answers typically range anywhere from "My child doesn't like books at all" to "My child could sit and look at books for hours." Children actually go through stages of interest when it comes to books and story time. Determining your child's stage of interest in books will help you discover how you can turn books and story time into interaction time.

Types of Books

Before we get into the specific stages, we need to talk about the types of books that are the most effective. If your child can destroy any book she comes in contact with in a matter of seconds, through ripping, biting, throwing, and so on, your job is to find the most indestructible books possible. Board books and foam books are good, but not destruction proof. The best books I have found for children who are really rough on books are made of thick fabric, also known as cloth books. If you are skilled with a sewing machine you can make your own. I have also found some really fun ones on the Internet (through E-bay or Google, to be precise).

Interactive. These are books that have buttons, flaps, tabs, and so on. Interactive books are fun sensory experiences for most children. You push the button and the train makes a noise, or you lift the flap and, "wow," there is a great picture. The aspect I like the best about interactive books is that you can help a child take a clear turn with an interactive book. You can push buttons and lift flaps together. The buttons and flaps also give a child something to do instead of just listening to words, which can be difficult for some when it comes to story time.

Repetitive. Repetitive books are also a great tool. Books that have patterns are easier to follow, and children can learn to predict what will come next. The rhythmic pattern that we tend to use when we read these types of stories almost makes them musical in nature. Children and grown-ups alike start to tap and sway to the beat of the story, thereby creating a sensory experience to accompany the story. One of the best known examples of this type of book is Eric Carle's *Brown Bear, Brown Bear*.

Special events. Many books have been written about the first day of school, a new baby sibling being born, moving to a new house, and so on. I find these books very helpful when teaching and preparing children for new experiences. I have a couple of favorites, including *Little Critter Books* by Mercer Mayer and the *Berenstain Bears* series by Jan and Stan Berenstain, that I use for the first day of school, going to the doctor and going to the dentist. I often shorten the text and personalize the story by inserting the child's name wherever possible, making it even more meaningful.

If I can't find a story to fit the specific event I am looking for, I make up my own. I tend to follow Carol Gray's format for Social Stories™ (2002) when I create personalized stories. That is, I include a descriptive statement that is *fact-based* and tells a child precisely what is going on. I then move on to a *directive statement* so that a child knows what his or her role in the event might be. It is also helpful to include *perspective statements* so a child will have support in understanding what others think and how others feel. I highly recommend using personalized stories whenever new events or difficult activities are on the horizon. I always write the story from the child's perspective and include pictures whenever I can. In Chapter 7 we will look more at Social Stories™.

A mom did a brilliant job creating a story for her son about trips to the store. She took him to the store and took actual photographs of the events as they occurred: getting out of the car, getting into a cart, walking up and down the aisles, holding a special toy, checking out, leaving the cart, getting into the car seat, and so on. She then put all the pictures into a small flip photo album and wrote a story to go with it. The story was simple and *described* exactly what was happening in the pictures. She also gave her child specific *directions* of what was acceptable behavior during each task. Finally, she threw in some *perspective statements* about how everyone would feel after a positive trip to the store. The story has become an all-time favorite and even better than that – Mom reported that trips to the store are no longer a nightmarish expedition.

Classics. Of course, when talking about books we can't leave out the classics: *Goldilocks and the Three Bears, The Three Little Pigs, Little Red Riding Hood,* and so on. These stories are great because of the social aspects they incorporate. Entire preschool classrooms have been known to focus on classic story themes for weeks at a time. The stories are incorporated into the classroom during pretend play, art activities, outside stage performances, and so on. These stories also appear in multiple preschool and kindergarten classrooms across the world, so helping your child become familiar with classic stories helps your child join in with his or her peers when she goes to school.

Story Time Stage

Now that we have discussed numerous types of books and stories, it is time to discuss the specific stages of story time – MINE!, Quick Flip, Label and Comments and Read to Me!

MINE! The first stage children typically go through is the MINE! stage. During this stage children have a very limited interest in books and the interest they do have does not include you. During the MINE! stage children tend to look at the cover of a book or flip through one or two pages at lightening speed. If you attempt to hold the book and read it to the child, it becomes their signal to leave the interaction entirely. At this stage children occasionally will lift a flap or push a button in an interactive book but, again, their interest is very limited.

So how can you help a MINE! stage child allow you to interact with her during book time? The key is to give up control and allow the child control. As grown-ups we tend to want to hold the book, turn the pages and read the entire story word for word, cover to cover. But at this stage, that type of interaction isn't going to cut it. First and foremost, let the child hold the book (yes, I know it's hard). Then position yourself in front of her, down at her level so you can watch her eyes to see what she looks at in the book.

Your next job is to simply make a comment about something that the child glances at in the book. Remember this is a child who will be looking at maybe one or two things in total, so you may only get one or two comments in. Even so, your comments should be relevant to the child's interests and full of life. If the only word that you get to say during the entire book is "Dora," then make it the most enthusiastic word you can muster. If you try the above steps and your child still doesn't have any interest in letting you in, try including something that does interest him.

> Some children prefer to sit in your lap for story time and don't like when the set-up of story time changes. If that is the case with your child, try reading in front of mirrored closet doors or a reflective surface so you can still see what it is in the book that interests the child.

Follow the child's lead by focusing on books that have characters he is interested in. My child loves *Dora the Explorer* or *The Wiggles*, so I get figurines of those characters to introduce during book time. Sometimes I start to "read" the book myself by opening the pages and having the figurines dance across the pages. Or I wait until my daughter looks at the book and then make the figurine dance around the book or next to the book. I often sing songs that the characters would sing during their television show to catch my child's interest.

Some families have created books that contain photographs of their child and family members. You can create short songs or rhythmic chants to name each person as you flip the pages of the book. I worked with a mom once who created a mini scrapbook using photographs of all of her child's favorite things – favorite toy, favorite food, favorite movie, favorite character, and so on. It was a big hit.

The key at the MINE! stage is to enter into the child's world slowly and unobtrusively. Focus on the child's interests and help him discover the fun parts of story time. You need to be an enthusiastic and exciting element that your child becomes motivated by as opposed to something he is threatened by, "Oh no, she might take my book away!" Once your child is showing more of an interest in books and allows you to join with him briefly, you can head into the next stage.

If using photographs, make sure they do not have a lot of background details that can be distracting.

Quick flip stage. During the Quick Flip stage children tend to look at the book in its entirety, but the whole book may only take seconds to flip through. I still allow the child to maintain control of the book by holding it and turning the pages; all I do is point to accompany my comment. That is, whereas previously I didn't intrude on the physical space of the book, I now gently point to an item I am commenting on. When I see the child excited about something on a page, I follow her lead and make it a ton of fun. The pages still flip pretty quickly, but I can comment and point to more and more things as the child finds me a fun and motivating partner.

If the book is interactive and has flaps or buttons (which I highly recommend), you have a couple of options. If your child pushes a button, you can imitate the sound or word the button action makes. If your child is not interested in pushing buttons or lifting flaps, you can push the button or lift the flap yourself and enthusiastically comment on what you see or hear. Remember not to take over too much, though. Your child should still feel very much in control of the interaction. You are just an added bonus that makes it even more fun!

Label and comments stage. Once a child allows me to intrude a bit on the book by pointing and joining in with the flaps and buttons, we are entering the next stage, Label and Comments. I pointed and commented on pictures in the book in the previous stage, but now the child becomes the one who labels things he is excited about. At this stage children start to anticipate me labeling something in the book, so I *Watch & Wait* even longer to give them an opportunity to label something themselves. I point and then say nothing. If a prompt becomes necessary, I start with the least intrusive, giving them a partial prompt of the word I am going for. I still follow their lead and focus on the pictures I know they are the most interested in but slip a turn in as well. Their turn becomes labeling objects in the book.

There are so many great books that include actual photographs of objects. I tend to gravitate to those books because the photographs help with receptive understanding and children are more likely to associate the photograph with the real object.

Great opportunities for back-and-forth turn taking often surface during the Label and Comments stage. I point to a picture and the child labels it; the child points to a picture and I label it, and so on. Many great skills are introduced and discovered during this type of interaction.

After the back-and-forth flow of the labeling has become very comfortable for the child, the comment portion of this stage becomes the focus. If a child points to a picture of a dog, I first label it, but then I can also add a comment, "A dog says woof" or "The dog is brown." In this way I am expanding on the child's interests and teaching different attributes that go with the object. At the same time I begin to extend the interaction from simple one-word labels to longer sentences – and soon the concept of a story starts to take shape.

Read to me! At this stage, reading a whole story is much more feasible. It has taken some baby steps to get here, but typically children now start to pay attention to books for longer periods of time. It is still important to think about what is motivating and try to follow the child's lead when choosing books. I also try to find books with a predictable and familiar routine so a child has clear opportunities to take a turn. Eric Carle's *Brown Bear, Brown Bear* is a perfect example.

When you start, begin by reading the first sentence, then pause before the last word in the sentence and prompt your child with a *"raised-eyebrow wait."* Wait a sufficient length of time to give the child an opportunity to take a turn. If this prompt is not enough to get the child to say the last word, you can point to the picture of the word you want him to say or give him a *partial prompt* by offering up the first sound of the word. You can continue the same pattern as you move through the book, pausing before the last word of each sentence and prompting when necessary.

As illustrated, it is important to find books that have a repetitive predictable routine so that children will have more opportunities for success when taking their turn. Children start to enjoy "reading" and learn to enjoy books when they get to participate in the story telling.

Visual Supports

Book time also offers great opportunities to add visual supports. As mentioned, I have had quite a bit of success looking stories up on the Internet to find flannel board patterns, coloring sheets, sequence worksheets, and so on, that I have used to create visual supports. I typically go to www.google.com and type in the name of a story using quotations around the name (e.g., "Brown Bear Brown Bear"). I then type a + sign and add the words "flannel board."

For example, I have found great patterns for stories like *The Very Hungry Caterpillar, Chicka Chicka Boom Boom, Old Macdonald Had a Farm, There was an Old Lady Who Swallowed a Fly,* and the list goes on. I print the pictures out on a piece of cardstock, color

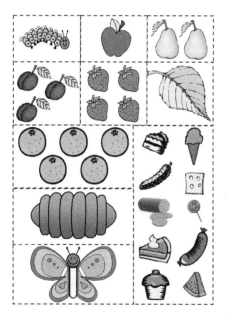

them, laminate them, add a hook piece of velcro to the back and soon have a fun flannel board story. You can also find great visual supports for children's books at teacher supply stores. Of course, you can make your own or cut them out of magazines, and so on.

Once you have the visual supports, you have to decide how you expect the child to take her turn. Maybe you decide to use the *keeper* strategy and that the child's turn will consist of taking pieces from you while you read the story and placing them on a flannel board (flannel aprons are fun, too). Or maybe the child will have to choose the piece that signifies what comes next in the story when you hold up two possibilities. You can also *make a mistake on purpose* by handing the child the wrong piece and giving her a chance to problem solve. Or you can *offer parts not wholes* by purposefully taking out all the pieces to *Brown Bear Brown Bear* except the blue horse, again providing the child with an opportunity to problem solve. Visual supports are fun and help increase children's understanding and love of books.

Read to Me! Once children get to this phase, it is a great time to create books about situations they experience. To do so, take photographs of your child doing various daily activities such as shopping, riding the bus, going to therapy, going swimming, and so on. Then write the story to describe what is happening in the pictures. Many parents use this technique when their children struggle with a particular life situation to teach them how they can act and respond when the situation occurs (based on the concept of Social Stories™ by Carol Gray). One mom I worked with created a story about moving across the country to a new house to help her son deal with all the changes involved in the family's move. She took pictures of the moving van, boxes, airplanes and the new house, and then created a story for her son to read.

Books can be very powerful tools once children learn to enjoy them. It is important to help them on their journey as they enter into the world of story time. Stories can also encourage pretend play as children progress through the reading stages. Just as children progress through stages of interest with books, they also progress through different stages of development in play. Pretend play and other play skills often don't come easy to children with ASD but as we will see in Chapter 6, there are many effective and fun ways to teach such skills.

Play and Toys Are Children's Work

You might have wondered why I waited until now to discuss toys. There is a reason for this. For many children on the spectrum, toys are tricky to navigate and often cause a variety of atypical behaviors. Whether it's the sensory stimulation they receive from continually spinning the wheels on a truck or the comfort they find in repetitively lining up a group of dinosaurs, children with ASD tend to struggle when it comes down to finding appropriate ways to play with toys.

Toys can initially get in the way of interactions. Now you may be saying, "Wait a minute, hasn't she already said we are supposed to follow the child's lead? If my child wants to line up dinosaurs or spin wheels on a truck, then I should join in and do the same!" The simple answer here is "yes" you should absolutely follow your child's lead and try spinning another wheel on the truck or get a truck of your own and spin the wheels or add your own dinosaur to the line-up. Following your child's lead so your child wants to interact with you is still an imperative part of helping your child progress.

But there is a more complex answer to the question. Play has an important role in children's physical, social, emotional, language and cognitive development and reinforces neural connections. That is, children who are deprived of play display fewer neural connections, thereby causing a biological regression of brain growth (Brown, Sutterby, & Thornton, 2001). Play, therefore, is a vital learning experience for all children. So although it is important to start out following your child's lead when you first begin to interact with the toys your child is interested in, it is necessary to teach the child how to play with a variety of toys.

Types of Toys

Before I discuss strategies you can use to help your child learn to play with toys, I will give a brief overview of the different kinds of toys that are available. Toys are designed for different stages of a child's development and are meant to help your child progress through the various stages.

Cause-and-effect toys. These toys allow a child to "cause" some type of reaction: Push a button and music plays, twist a knob and a toy jumps out, kick a panel and lights flash, and so on. Cause-and-effect toys are often found in the infant and toddler sections of toy stores. They help children learn to pay attention to a specific object as they become interested in seeking out the "effect." These toys also help children begin to develop skills of anticipation as they more purposefully cause the action that brings about the desired effect. Cause-and-effect toys continue to be relevant past the stages of infant and toddler development. For example, a TV remote control is a very useful (and often powerful) cause-and-effect toy.

Visual-spatial toys. This type of toy has a built-in structure that a child is able to follow visually. Shape sorters, for example, are visual-spatial toys. When playing with a shape sorter, a child places the square shape into the square hole, the circle shape into the circle hole, and so on. Puzzles are another example of a visual spatial toy. The letter "A" puzzle piece always goes into the "A" spot on the alphabet puzzle. Ring stackers also fall into this category. A ring goes onto the stick of the ring stacker. A child can visually see the appropriate space for the toy to fit.

While many visual-spatial toys have only one "correct" place where a given piece fits, they can include things like stringing beads where many different combinations may be attempted. Visual-spatial toys help children develop eye-hand coordination as well as the ability to match items. If a child places a piece incorrectly, she learns about the concept of trial and error as she attempts to place the piece in different locations in search of the perfect fit. When a child does figure out the correct space that a piece can fit into, it can become very reinforcing to find the correct space again and again. Children with ASD are very visual learners and visual-spatial toys often become a strength and even a favorite.

Construction toys. These toys take the concept of visual-spatial toys to the next level. Instead of each piece having a specific and constant space, pieces of construction toys may be placed more freely throughout the structure – think Legos, blocks, Lincoln Logs, Tinker Toys, and so on. When playing with construction toys, balance and motion become more of an issue as builders attempt to construct taller and more elaborate structures. Children must learn to implement planning strategies in order to successfully complete a desired structure. They also must learn to problem solve in a variety of ways when playing with construction toys. Pieces of different sizes, lengths and widths can add to the structure, or hinder the development if they are placed incorrectly. A piece may not fit where it was originally intended, so the ability to demonstrate flexibility of thought comes into play as design plans must be changed.

Individual pretend play. Also called imaginative play, this involves important skills. Before children can develop pretend play skills within a group, they need to develop pretend play on their own. In pretend play children demonstrate their use of imitation skills. Children may imitate a teacher teaching or a grocery clerk checking out groceries.

The first scripts children tend to act out are scripts that they are familiar with. If you have a new baby in the house, pretend play with a doll is something you would expect to see. Your child may imitate cooking routines, shopping for groceries, going to school – the possibilities are endless. Children begin to develop a sense of the world as they explore a variety of scenarios in play routines – visits to the doctor, going to a restaurant, building a house, and so on.

The important thing is to provide the tools the child will need to practice her imaginative play skills. Pint-size versions of grown-up activities are the best toys to have around. For a pretend play activity focused around cooking, plastic food and dishes need to be available. If your child loves construction vehicles, be sure to include small construction vehicles with dirt and rocks to move around as part of his toy collection. Many great toys are available to support pretend play scripts, so have fun finding the toys that are motivating for your child.

Pretend play with peers. Once children are demonstrating pretend play skills on their own, it is time to move into pretend play with peers. As children expand their creativity and imagination by adding peers to their pretend play, they learn to compromise, organize, share thoughts and ideas, take turns, and so on. But most important, especially for children on the autism spectrum, they begin to learn to interact socially and form positive peer relationships.

Games with rules. This type of game is another important part of children's development. Learning that other people like to take turns and like to win is a huge step in developing the ability to think about what peers and family members think and feel – a challenge for most children with ASD.

Learning to play games with rules allows children to explore a variety of interests and develop friendships with peers who share their interests as game play develops and advances. Games also provide children with opportunities to plan strategies and problem solve to further their position in the game. Of equal importance, games with rules help us learn about a variety of emotions, from disappointment and sadness to pride and joy.

Learning to play games with rules is an important social, emotional and cognitive goal. Children with ASD have a difficult time with these games because they feel very strongly about winning and lack the "theory of mind" or perspective-taking skills (Winner, 2002) to understand that someone else might like to win, too. They also struggle to appropriately express their frustration with losing and may react impulsively and even inappropriately when they lose.

Strategies for Helping Children Learn to Play

Now that we have looked at stages and categories of toys and some of the important goals that children need to learn at each stage, let's explore strategies you can incorporate to help your child learn to play.

One of the tools that I have used for years in private therapy is video modeling. Video modeling is a research-based tool (e.g., Corbett, 2003) that promotes play behaviors in a format that is motivating and attention holding for children with ASD. The *Teach Me to Play* DVD (Cardon, 2007) depicts children playing appropriately with a variety of toys at each developmental stage and, therefore, can be used to help your child learn to play with toys. Video modeling promotes appropriate play behaviors free from reliance on other people, which in turn means less chance for prompt dependency. A child who is less prompt dependent in play can initiate play on his own. And a child who can play appropriately and independently becomes free to focus on interactions with peers that can promote socialization.

When helping a child learn how to play, it is important to think back to the strategies we discussed in Chapter 1. *Watch & Wait* to see what toys your child appears to be interested in. Maybe there is a theme to the items she is attracted to. Maybe the child likes every toy that has wheels or every toy that has a particular character associated with it. Maybe there is a sensory component involved in the toy play, and she likes every toy that spins or lights up.

Remember, you want your child to play with toys because of the important developmental milestones toys help children achieve. At the same time, you want your child to play with toys because of the great interaction opportunities they promote. Toy time is a chance for grown-ups to be silly and fun and let their hair down. It is also a great time to establish an emotional connection with your child. So think about the stage of play your child needs to start with and create some fun and motivating interactions. As always, teach your child how and when to take his turn.

It is always a good idea to start with things the child already finds motivating. Chances are that if you observe carefully, you will discover the things your child is interested in and will be able to find toys that are motivating. Once you have found those toys, the goal is to make playing tons of fun.

The strategies that were introduced in Chapter 2 can help you create great interactions when you and your child play with toys. The fun interactions will help your child stay motivated to play and your involvement will help the child learn how to play with the toy appropriately. Let's talk about the stages of play and how the different strategies might look at each stage.

Cause-and-effect toys. As mentioned, when it comes to cause-and-effect toys, the reinforcing and motivating source is often built right in. You may just need to help the child learn how to successfully take her turn, after that the lights and sounds coming from the toy are usually motivation enough for the child to want to try again. A physical prompt may be necessary the first couple of times. Introducing a variety of cause-and-effect toys with buttons to push and knobs to pull, twist and turn helps your child develop better hand-eye coordination and the ability to move on to visual-spatial toys.

Visual-spatial toys. These toys often have multiple parts. Therefore, a natural strategy to use would be the *keeper* strategy. Take a shape sorter, for example. Give the child one or two pieces to get started with. Be sure the child has plenty of time to explore the toy on his own; if he is not at all interested, play with the toy yourself, making sure that your excitement and enthusiasm for the toy shine through. If the child seems interested but has difficulty putting the shape in, provide a physical prompt to help him be successful.

Children who have not yet developed verbal skills can take their turns in a variety of ways. They can use a picture card to exchange for the shape, they can point to the shape (remember you can physically help them learn to do this if they have not learned the skill yet), they can sign "more" to get the shape, they can produce a verbalization that you can then interpret as their asking for more, and so on. The key is that you need to determine what an appropriate turn would

*Some shape sorters have so many different shapes that it can be overwhelming. If that is the case, you can tape over some of the shapes and only focus on one or two shapes at a time. Remember, in the beginning stages we don't want the child to feel overwhelmed. From there on you can employ the **keeper** strategy.*

be for your child. If your child is verbal but not initiating verbally, you can use a partial prompt, "shhhhhhh____," to encourage him to say the word "shape" or "ssssssss____" to prompt the word "circle." Maybe your child can produce multiple-word sentences but struggles with initiation, regardless, your prompt needs to include as much *Watch & Wait* time as possible. Then you can move to an "I want _____," partial prompt.

Several families have been successful writing the words "I want _____" on a card to help their child ask for more of something. They direct their child's attention to the card with a look or a point to encourage the child to ask "I want ____."

If your child has lots of words and is frequently initiating, you can employ the *keeper* strategy but with an added twist. Encourage the child to verbally make a choice between two different shapes or two like shapes of different colors. You can also *make a mistake on purpose* and give the child the wrong shape once she has made a request. That way, you allow the child an opportunity to problem solve to get the piece he requested. Some children don't protest when they are given the wrong piece; help them learn how to protest appropriately and get their needs met. These ideas don't just apply to shape sorters; you can use them with most visual-spatial toys – ring stackers, puzzles, beads, and so on.

Once your child has begun to find shape sorters and other visual-spatial toys interesting, you can use the *jarful of fun* strategy. Get a large plastic jar and place some of the pieces of the toy inside. As always, you have set up a reason for the child to initiate and interact with you. The child has to bring the jar to you, and request help opening the jar by, for example, placing your hand on the jar, saying "open" or any number of things to get access to the pieces inside. Also try *parts not wholes;* you can lay out the shapes but not the shape sorter, or the puzzle pieces but no puzzle board. I often hide the missing piece under a cloth in the room so that we can play *hide and seek* together before we play with the visual spatial toy. The key is to make play fun so it becomes motivating for your child!

Strategy	You can try . . .
Be the keeper	Offering one piece at a time.
Jarful of fun	Placing some or even all of the pieces in a jar and screw the lid on tight. Teach your child how to request for the pieces.
Hide-n-seek	Hiding the pieces under a cloth or chair, in a bag, behind a door; search together to find them.
Parts not wholes	Placing the pieces out but not the receptacle. Or put the receptacle out without any pieces. Guide the child through the process to determine what she needs.
Make a mistake on purpose	Giving your child the wrong piece when he makes a request. Teach him to how to get the piece he really wants.

Construction toys. When it comes to playing with construction toys, you can use some of the strategies that were just mentioned. For example, you can be the keeper of the Legos or the blocks and teach the child how to take a turn in requesting them. You can have a *jarful of fun* and place pieces in a large plastic jar to encourage initiation. Sometimes it is fun to build the tallest tower you can and then take great pleasure in crashing it to the ground. The crashing-down part can be very motivating and reinforcing. It is also a fun time to be silly and really captivate your child's interest.

For children who get interested in building specific projects, it is helpful to build a structure ahead of time and then take a picture of it. I use the picture as a visual support, which helps children get a clear idea in their heads; besides, it serves as a reference as we build. When playing with construction toys, follow the child's lead and include favorite characters, toys or special interests. You can create a dog house for Blue (*Blue's Clues*) or a pirate ship for Captain Feathersword (*The Wiggles*). You can also build a house for a favorite stuffed animal as one more way to make the play motivating and fun.

Individual pretend play. Greenspan and Wieder (1998) recommend that we follow the *ideas* in children's play. Don't be afraid to let your child's ideas guide pretend play. If my child wants to pretend that a shape sorter bucket is a hat or a drum, I follow her lead and join in instead of trying to insist that we use an actual hat. It is important to support pretend play by really knowing what the child is interested in. If Bob the Builder is a favorite, have some Bob the Builder stuffed animals, puppets, construction equipment, and so on, available so the child has a familiar script to work from. If the child loves Disney movies, have toys available to support pretend play themed around a favorite movie.

As adults we often forget the way we played as children and become much more guarded in our play. Be sure that you have some good, typical models to help you to remember how to pretend.

Grown-ups tend to get nervous about aggressive play or play with negative themes. However, it is important to support a child in exploring feelings and emotions as a part of his or her life experiences. Children explore feelings and emotions through play; for example, a battle ensues and a knight is stabbed; a dinosaur eats a Barbie doll; an airplane crashes into a building, and so on. While these play themes sometimes make grown-ups uncomfortable, children are often trying to understand and make sense of their world through pretend play. This type of play is an acceptable expression of anger and aggression, two areas that children on the spectrum tend to have difficulty expressing appropriately.

Finally, it is also important to expand children's life experiences so they can expand their pretend play experiences: trips to the grocery store, the zoo, a doctor, a restaurant, a train depot, and the list go on.

Pretend play with peers. Pamela Wolfberg, author of *Peer Play and the Autism Spectrum* (2005), has developed an innovative program for providing support to children during peer play. Expert players and novice players gather together and with the support of a facilitator learn to interact and play together. Children on the spectrum are considered the novice players and are paired with expert players. The goals of an Integrated Play Group are to foster spontaneous, mutually enjoyed play among peers. Integrated Play Groups also help children expand and diversify their symbolic play. The play groups incorporate structured routines and visual supports, thereby tapping into preferred learning styles and areas of strength for children with ASD.

Don't expect your child to jump through the stages of play over night. It may (and should) take time to explore toys at each stage. The lessons children learn at each stage are essential to their growth and development. When children are able to progress through stages of play and develop the ability to pretend, they are nurturing their ability to think in abstract ways. Children's imaginations grow and help them think beyond the here and now. This is a critical element in developing theory of mind, or the ability to put oneself in someone else's shoes and think about how others think – a major challenge for children with ASD. Theory of mind is a critical skill in developing effective communication skills and building strong relationships throughout life, making it all the more important to work on these areas.

CHAPTER 7

Visual Supports
Every Day in Every Way

Throughout this book I have referred to a variety of visual supports. In fact, I debated whether or not this chapter should come at the beginning because visual supports are so critical to assisting children with ASD. It ended up here, however, because until you fully understand the concept of helping your child learn how and when to initiate, visual supports won't be as effective.

Some families are very nervous about incorporating visual supports every day in every way when they first come to see me. They think that a child who uses pictures will never learn to talk. I have found the very opposite to be true and I am not alone in that assessment (Frost & Bondy, 2002). Visual supports are very effective for children with ASD because they tend to be strong visual learners. Information that is only presented auditorily – information that is spoken – is much more difficult for them to comprehend, process and act upon. Visual supports help words and ideas become permanent (Sussman, 1999). That is, children understand information better because they don't have to guess what we really mean as there's a concrete picture right in front of them.

An added bonus is that visual supports help us as grown-ups to be clear and precise in our presentation of information. We have to organize ourselves more in order to present information visually. When we organize our ideas and thoughts, we become easier to understand. For example, during a one-hour speech session I use visual supports so that the child knows exactly what to expect during that hour. When I set up the visual supports I have to organize the materials that I will need and really think about the goals that I hope to achieve during each session. The session goes much more smoothly because I have prepared everything carefully ahead of time and the child and I know what to expect.

Why Use Visual Supports?
1. Children with ASD are strong visual learners.
2. Visual information is easier to comprehend, process and act upon.
3. Visual supports help ideas and words become permanent.
4. Children with ASD understand visually presented information better.
5. Adults who use visual supports communicate more clearly and precisely.

You may be thinking, "Well, visual supports aren't important for my child because my child already knows how to talk." Let's be honest, most adults I know rely heavily on visual supports – Blackberries, Palm Pilots, daily planners, and so on. The truth is that everyone uses visual supports. The extent and degree to which we use those supports may vary, but *everyone* uses visual supports in some way or another. In short, visual supports are appropriate for children who are nonverbal, children who have emerging verbal skills and children who are considered advanced verbal communicators.

Where to Find Visuals

Now that we have established the importance of using visual supports, let's talk about where to begin. The first step is to determine what type of visual supports will be the most beneficial for your child. Too often I walk into a classroom and see the same pictures being used for every child. That is like saying "okay, all grown-ups have to use the same calendar system." It doesn't make sense. In addition, it is important to choose pictures that are of high quality.

The following hierarchy (Mirenda & Locke, 1989) that can help you determine what types of visuals to use for your child. However, remember that there is no "one size fits all" for children with ASD, so this hierarchy is meant only as a guide. The first level in the hierarchy is actual *objects*. If you want to teach your child what a goldfish cracker is, then use an actual goldfish cracker. If your child is learning what a sock is, use an actual sock.

Visual Supports Hierarchy

1. Objects
2. Color photographs
3. Black & white photographs
4. Color line drawings
5. Black & white line drawings
6. Written word

From P. Mirenda & P. Lock, 1989, A comparison of symbol transparency in nonspeaking persons with intellectual abilities. Journal of Speech and Hearing Disorders, 54, *131-140.*

If your child tends to do well when using various objects, the next level in the hierarchy may be a more appropriate starting place. *Color photographs* of objects, people, and so on, are great visual supports to use for many children. In this age of digital cameras, using photographs has gotten easier than ever to use for this purpose.

I have found some very helpful software known as *Picture This* (Silver Lining Multimedia, 2000) that contains over 5,000 color photographs. One of my favorite color photograph tricks I discovered on the Internet. The website www.google.com has a search tool known as "images." Just go to the site and click on the word "images" (you will find it directly above the search box). Then type in any word you want and, when possible, Google will provide you with color photos of the item you are searching for. I tend to start at the color photograph level. If a child struggles at this level, then I back up and use objects.

> Be aware, some children get very stuck on the specific object in the photograph. For example, if the photograph shows the blue sippy cup, your child may only want juice in the blue sippy cup.

Next in the line-up come *black and white photographs*. To be honest, I rarely use black and white photographs because most of the children I work with transition to the next stage, *color line drawings*, without needing to go through black and whites.

Color line drawings are often readily available in educational settings. I have also run across some great software programs that incorporate color line drawings and help create visual supports (*Writing With Symbols*, Mayer Johnson, 2000).

> Success has been found using black-and-white line drawings when the word label is consistently paired with the picture symbol. So please remember to pair the spoken word with picture symbols to aid in your child's comprehension (Harris & Reichle, 2004).

Next are *black and white line drawings*. There are some great websites where you can find free black and white line drawings (for example, do2learn.com), and in a pinch you can always grab a pen and try drawing one yourself. No artistic talent is required!

The final level in the hierarchy is the *written word*. My goal is always to help children progress through the stages so that they get to the point where written words are enough to do the trick. Not all children will get to this level, but the goal is always there.

Speaking of written words, I suggest always placing the written word with the picture. There are a couple of reasons for this.

First, if you have several different people interacting with your child throughout the day, it is important that everyone uses the same terminology to refer to the objects in the pictures. Take the example of the sippy cup picture. One person may look at that picture and say "sippy cup," another may look at it and say "drink" while a third may come along and label it "juice." How is a child going to learn the label for the object in the picture if everyone is referring to it differently?

Second, we all use visual supports; however, the most socially acceptable form of visual supports as we get older is the written word. I always place the written word with a picture, and as the child's skill level increases, the picture gets smaller while the word becomes the main focus until eventually the goal is met and the child is using only the written word and the picture has been faded out completely.

What to Support Visually

Now that you have ideas on how and where to get great photographs and pictures, it is important to decide what the visual supports are supposed to be supporting. Visual supports can and should help with both receptive and expressive language.

Receptive language refers to understanding language. Children have a better chance of understanding information when it is presented clearly and precisely. Visual supports that aid with receptive communication help children understand what is happening to them and their world because of the clear way in which the information is presented.

Expressive language involves the production or output of language in order to communicate with others. Expressive language may be verbal or nonverbal. Children who are nonverbal may use visual supports as their primary method of expressive communication. Children with emerging verbal skills may use visuals to jumpstart their processing to help them determine and initiate information they want to convey. Finally, children with more advanced verbal skills may use visual supports to aid them in expressing feelings and emotions or even to help maintain topics in conversations and participate in turn taking.

Receptive Visual Support

Receptive visual supports come in many different forms, but the main purpose behind them is to help children *understand what is happening to them and around them.* Too often we try to have children switch from activity to activity only to be met with resistance (or as I often hear them referred to: "meltdowns"). Resistance comes for several reasons, but one of the biggest reasons is that children don't understand where we are taking them or why we are asking them to shift from one activity to the next. Too often we are directing children and not including them in the process. *Receptive visual supports are one way to ensure that children are included.*

Choice boards. One way to include children is to let them know what choices are available – what's on the menu, so to speak. You can present them with visuals that literally tell them what's on the menu when you create food choice boards.

You can also create choice boards to help a child know what activities are available to choose from.

Limit the number of choices that you present. And, as always, remember to *teach your child how and when to take his turn.*

Most children do not know what to do with visual supports the first several times they are presented with them, so a physical prompt is often necessary. You also have to decide what is the most advantageous way to use the visual support. Maybe you want the child to see what choices are available (receptive language) and then move into expressive language by having the child point to or pull off the choice she is making.

If I am going to be using a picture exchange system (see page 70 for more detail) with a child, I usually prompt the child to pull the picture off and hand it to me to request what she wants. Choice boards are very helpful in letting children know what toys they can play with or what videos they can watch. All children – whether they are nonverbal, have emerging verbal skills, or are fairly confident verbal communicators – benefit from knowing what their options are. Start with one or two choices, and as children gain a clear understanding of the pictures, offer more choices.

You can also use choice boards to help children know what sensory activities they can choose from. Have an object choice board available so they can make a choice and receive the sensory input they need almost immediately. During therapy sessions I even use choice boards to help children see the songs that we are going to be singing that day. Then I let them take control and choose the order in which we sing each song. By offering the song choices I can be sure that the goals the child needs to meet are being represented by specific songs, while helping the child feel empowered because he gets to have a say in what is going on.

Before we go any further, let's talk about how to let a child know when something is NOT a choice or isn't a choice any longer. For example, if a child is very motivated by cookies, he may not understand when a cookie choice is no longer available. Let's say he has already eaten five cookies or that there are no more cookies left. I introduce a universal "no" symbol with the word "no" written under it and teach the child what the symbol means. I offer a picture of the cookie choice but then limit the number of cookies by only having two or three in a see-through jar set in plain view of the child. Once the cookies are not an option any more, I place the universal "no" symbol over the picture of the

cookies. I also try to quickly provide another very motivating food or activity as a positive distracter. Once I have shown a child that "cookie" is no longer a choice, I remove it from the choice board. Be forewarned: You will not always be the most popular person when the cookie is no longer available as a choice. However, it is an important life lesson that we must help children learn – let's just do it in the most positive way we can.

First/then board. While you may have to take away the cookie choice, you can let a child know what's going to happen next by using a first/then board. Place a picture of the cookie on the "first" side of the board by using velcro or magnets and put another very motivating activity on the "then" side of the board. Then state "*First* cookie, *then* movie." That way the child knows the world isn't going

to end when the cookie goes away. Once the cookie is done, remove the cookie picture from the board and focus on the movie picture.

> *One key thing to remember here: Be sure to use two reinforcing, positive rewards when you first introduce the board, "First cookie, then ice cream," for example. We want a child to establish a positive memory of the first/then board and not only associate it with things she hates to do.*

First/then boards are great supports for children at all stages of communication. If you think about it, the concept of first/then is also a great support for most adults. We often give ourselves mini goals to work toward, "*First* I will write ten pages and *then* I will reward myself by watching some television!" The same concept can work for our children. When you use a first/then board, you can help the child deal with activities that are not his favorites but still may be necessary such as teeth brushing or hand washing. "First brush teeth, then play."

Schedules. Letting the child know what comes next can be accomplished in several ways. You can use "mini-schedules" to let the child see what she will be doing over a short period of time or schedules that represent time frames as long as a day, week or even a month.

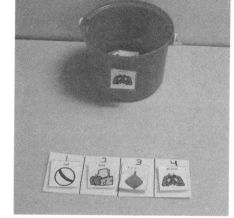

A mini schedule can represent three or four activities that are meant to take place over the course of an hour or over the course of twenty minutes. When you are using schedules, be sure to give the child a way to recognize that an activity is "finished" or "all done" by having a specific place to put the picture

such as a pocket or envelope, or by turning the picture over when the activity ends. The concept of checking off a to-do list comes to mind here. Remember the visual support hierarchy (page 59): If a child is struggling with color line drawings or photographs, try using an object schedule to show what comes next.

Daily schedules come in all kinds of shapes and sizes. The important thing is to find out what works best for the child. For example, some children do better with a schedule that is laid out vertically while others respond better to schedules that are laid out horizontally. *Watch & Wait* to determine what type of schedule is most beneficial for your child. If you have a vertical schedule up and your child never looks beyond the first two items, try converting it to a horizontal schedule.

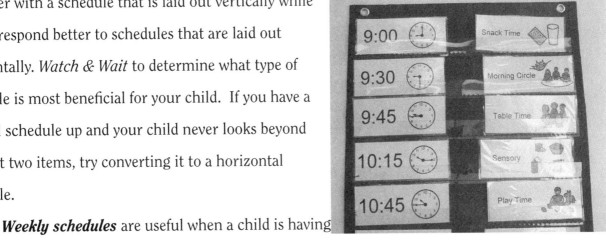

Weekly schedules are useful when a child is having a difficult time understanding when a specific event is coming up. For example, if your child wants to know which therapists she is going to see each day, create a weekly schedule with the picture of each person she will be visiting on the appropriate day of the week. Or if your child loves to go swimming but only gets to go to the pool on Saturdays, create a way for him to see how

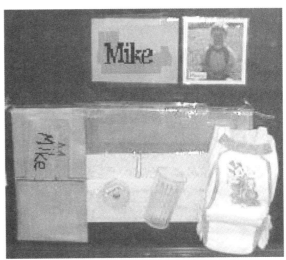

many school days or bed times it takes to get to Saturday.

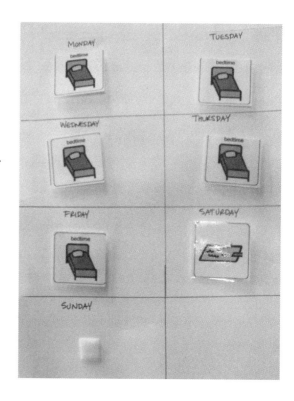

Even with schedules in place many children have difficulty shifting their attention from one activity to the next. For such cases I introduce **transition visual supports**. Transition visual supports can take many forms. Sometimes it is as simple as giving the child a real object to hold as he makes the transition to the next activity. For example, if you were transitioning to snack time, the child could hold the sippy cup as you walk from the family room to the kitchen. If a child has been playing well in a waiting room and has trouble transitioning back to a therapy room, consider using a *people locator* (picture of the person the child is about to go see that she can hold and carry into the therapy room) to help the child know who they are transitioning to.

I am a big believer in some sort of timer as a transition visual support. "Time Timers " (Copyright ©1999-2006 Time Timer, LLC) are very popular and work well with many children to help them know how much longer they have before a transition is about to take place. Some children respond well to a traditional egg timer.

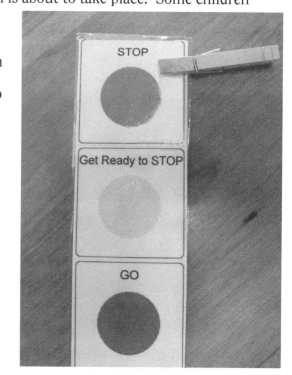

I also use a stop light system. The clothes pin is on green when the activity is in full swing. When it is time to think about stopping the activity, I move the clothespin to yellow, and when the activity is finished I place it on red. Some children like to move the clothespin themselves. This simple tool serves as a visual and tactile cue that the activity is going to be ending soon. Use a small wooden block in a similar fashion with sides painted red, yellow and green.

Self-help. Another type of receptive visual support helps children learn to do things more independently, including following the routines and self-help tasks that they are presented with on a daily basis.

Think about the routines your child participates in every day: dressing, pottying, diapering, eating, teeth brushing, bathing, and so on. These routines are perfect opportunities to increase your child's receptive understanding because they occur on a regular basis. As human beings we tend to be creatures of habit. For example, we tend to follow a morning routine that we get very used to. When we travel to a hotel or our alarm doesn't go off, our morning routine is interrupted and we may feel a bit thrown off and out of control.

Children react the same way when their routines are interrupted. We know that children on the spectrum respond well to structure and consistency, so creating visual supports to further the structure and consistency is a positive way to increase their receptive understanding and general well-being.

Self-help visual supports can take many different forms, depending on what the child responds best to. If your child struggles with the morning routine, provide a visual support and place everything she needs in a box so she can see exactly what is involved. If your child needs support with the steps of hand washing, place pictures of the individual steps right on the bathroom mirror.

> *In addition to setting up a transition system, teach children how it works so they can feel more secure as transitions and changes come. When children have an increased understanding of the situation, they tend to go into "meltdown mode" less and less.*

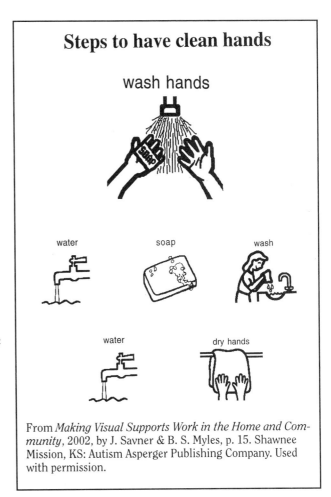

Steps to have clean hands

wash hands

water   soap   wash

water   dry hands

From *Making Visual Supports Work in the Home and Community*, 2002, by J. Savner & B. S. Myles, p. 15. Shawnee Mission, KS: Autism Asperger Publishing Company. Used with permission.

Or maybe you want your child to work on independently choosing clothing. Place pictures on drawers to indicate the clothing items she will find inside and create a picture list so that the child can match each picture up and find what she needs to get dressed.

To help your child take part in family routines like setting the table or prepare snacks, your child can start practicing with real dishes as you help him learn to take turns with a visual template. You can also use a visual template as the child moves into pretend play and sets the table with pretend dishes. To enable the child to make her own snacks, you

can set up a work station so the child has a starting point and an ending point.

Don't forget to help the child learn how and when (and in this case where) to take a turn so he doesn't get frustrated. Just setting out the workbox won't automatically mean that your child knows what to do with it. You may need to physically or verbally prompt the child through it the first couple of times. Remember *Watch & Wait* first to see if he can do it independently. Only then prompt, if needed.

Receptive visual supports are also beneficial when you are trying to help children understand what is expected of them in certain situations. For example, I worked with a boy who loved to repeat out loud the script of the computer game he was playing. The trouble was that he had headphones on and tended to repeat the script rather loudly, thereby interrupting the rest of the class. To address this concern I created a visual support to remind him what he was supposed to be doing.

Similarly, I have seen many parents use a stop sign to help their child learn to stop at the front or back door or stop before going into a sibling's room.

I have also helped families create visual supports to help their children learn to take turns. Put pictures of each child on a piece of foam core board during game play. Only the picture of the child taking a turn is visible at one time. The pictures prompt the appropriate turns and take away the child's dependency on verbal cues. One of the parents I worked with carried a key ring with pictures that she used to remind her son of what was expected of him on the go. In the grocery store she would show him a picture she had taken of him sitting nicely in the cart. In the parking lot she would show him a picture of the two of them holding hands. It was a great strategy because the mom didn't have to worry about her verbal instructions being misunderstood, which is particularly important when a child's safety is a concern.

If your child seems to be floundering because he is not sure what is expected of him, get creative and create a visual support so the abstract becomes more concrete.

Another family decided to create visual supports to encourage their child to participate in family routines. They set up a recycle station so their daughter could visually identify where the trash should go. I have seen many classrooms implement the very same strategy.

Receptive visual supports can also play a powerful role in assisting children in developing cognitive skills. Children with ASD are visual learners so we must teach them visually. I have seen many amazing tasks created to help children master a particular skill. One of my favorite resources is *Tasks Galore* (Eckenrode et al., 2005). The creators of *Tasks Galore* modeled the tasks in the book after the work stations they created and used while working with children on the spectrum.

Remember to create tasks that provide children with a clear visual field, a clear beginning and end, and a clear structure to follow. And as always, don't forget to *teach them how and when to take their turn.* With the category task a child may need physical support placing the animals in the appropriate space or may just need to see you actually do the task once or twice before she is ready to do it on her own. Some children only need verbal prompts, "Put the lion in the zoo." Some children could start the task based on a question or comment, "I wonder where the lion goes?" You can find many great tasks on the Internet just by typing in a few key words on a search engine.

One task I have used with multiple families involves teaching a child to spell his name using foam letters and a task box. Every child is different, of course, but I have had success demonstrating the task first by matching each foam letter to the name spelling and then placing it on a velcro square. With children who needed more support initially, I physically helped them match the letters and place them on the velcro. As a speech pathologist I have used task boxes to help children learn matching, categorizing, sorting by attributes and numerous other goals.

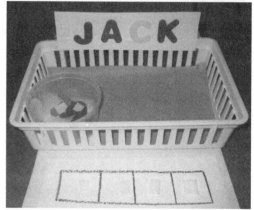

Expressive Visual Supports

While it is important for children to understand language and follow directions as expressed through receptive communication, expressive language is a powerful tool for formulating and subsequently getting one's needs met.

PECS. When it comes to expressive visual supports I highly recommend using a picture exchange system. The Picture Exchange Communication System (PECS) developed by Frost and Bondy (2002) is a great tool because it encourages initiation. Some people worry about using pictures for communication and think their children will become dependent on them. However, research on PECS (Frost & Bondy, 2002) indicates the opposite is true; that is, children's verbal language increases while their problem behaviors decrease when using PECS.

In my own practice I have found this to be true as well. Of course, that is not to say that pictures are the best modality for every child with autism; there is no "one size fits all." Some children I have worked with are amazing with sign language. Knowing that children with ASD are strong visual learners, however, pictures are a great place to start.

I will not go into great detail about how to implement a picture exchange system because you need support from a trained professional to do it correctly. Implementing PECS stage by stage is the best way I have found to teach a child how to initiate and discriminate what is on the picture cards. However, I must admit that I am not a strict PECS enforcer and have modified programs to fit a particular child. However, I never modify the initial three stages because they are key in helping a child be successful.

Once a child learns how to exchange pictures to express wants and needs, several visual tools can be used to support his "words." PECS encourages children to use large folders with velcro to house their pictures. Mini folders are more portable, and some children use a key ring system. They flip to the picture they want and then initiate with the entire key ring.

I have also seen parents turn choice boards into receptive and expressive visual supports. Choice boards still work receptively because they let the child know what choices are being offered, but parents then use picture exchange techniques to teach the child how to exchange the choice board pictures to get what she wants. For example, a parent may put three different snacks on a choice board so that a child knows what the options are. Instead of just watching a child point to the snack that he wants, use the stages of PECS to teach him how to bring you the picture of the snack that he chose.

Written cues. Another type of expressive visual support I use regularly is written cue. Written cues are particularly helpful when a child is a pretty good labeler but is having trouble moving beyond the labels. As noted previously, I do not expect a child to move to two-word combinations, and eventually sentences, until she is using fifty different words spontaneously. Once the child has reached this milestone, I introduce written visual cues to help expand utterances.

> Determine the system that works best for you and your child and stick to it. Your child's success depends on your consistency and follow-through.

For example, if a child uses cookie as one of his fifty words and has been successfully asking for cookie for some time, I write out the word "want" so that the next time he says "cookie" I show him the card, point to it, and say "want cookie." I then hand him the cookie. Notice I don't expect him to use the word "want" the first time he sees it. I am putting meaning to the card by expanding on what he already said. I also only point to the card when I say "want" so as not to make things confusing.

Written cues are not only appropriate for early readers. Many children learn what the card means because they consistently see and hear the word. Remember the turn-taking supports introduced to teach a child receptively when it was her turn? You can add the written cue "my turn" and teach the child how to use it as an expressive visual support as well. I often use a great program called *Writing With Symbols* (Mayer Johnson, 2000) to add pictures to the words. The pictures are color line drawings so they won't be appropriate for every child, but for the most part when the children I work with are ready to move to written cues, the color line drawings tend to do the trick.

I also use written cues to help children learn to ask "wh" questions, including what, when, where, who, and why. Once you have taught your child how and when to take his turn, he will be able to use a multitude of written cues.

To help children express what happened during their school day I encourage families and schools to set up a daily reporting system. I keep it pretty simple so a teacher is not overwhelmed with unreasonable demands and a child can pick up on the structure rather quickly. It typically looks something like this:

Sample Daily Report

Today in circle time we sang _____ .

Today I played with _____

Outside I _____ .

Tomorrow I will _____ .

Teachers fill in the four areas each day so that parents can guide their child through the ever-popular "What did you do at school today?" question. Parents can ask their children more specific questions such as, "What did you sing in circle time?" and after *Watching & Waiting* to see if the child needs help, they can prompt with a partial prompt or even interpret the answer directly because they will know the answer.

Parents can also structure their questions according to the answers the teacher has provided. Maybe one day it will be "Who did you play with today?" and another day it will be "What did you play with today?" This visual support is a good way to get some dialogue started with your child.

Emotions. The abstract nature of emotions makes them difficult for children with ASD not only to understand but also to express.

I use visual supports to teach children to receptively learn to understand emotions and also to express the emotions they are feeling. *Let's Talk Emotions* (Cardon, 2004) provides an array of ideas to help children learn to understand their emotions. It also introduces ways to help children express their emotions, including emotional thermometers and emotional journals. Emotional thermometers are particularly helpful when children get frustrated and have difficulty finding the words they need because they are so upset. The visual reminders and clarity an emotional thermometer lends them is invaluable in times like these. The Incredible 5-Point Scale developed by Kari Dun Buron and Mitzi Curtis (2004) offers another concrete, visual way of helping children identify and express emotions.

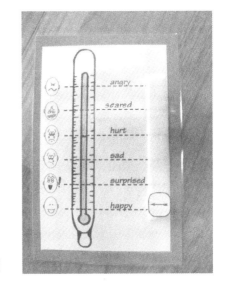

Social Stories™ (Gray, 2002) are another helpful tool for both receptive and expressive language. Social Stories are meant to provide children with the information they need to make good decisions about situations, along with validating the feelings they may have in those situations.

There are three main parts to a Social Story™. The first part is the *descriptive* portion of the story. You make a clear statement of fact, "I am going to build a Lego tower with my group." Then you provide a *directive statement* to help the child understand what to do (receptive). You can also provide the expressive support the child needs to help her determine what to say. "To build the tower I will need to ask for all the green pieces. I can say, 'Can I have the green pieces, please?'" (expressive). The final part is the *perspective statement*, "My group will feel happy because I asked nicely. I will be glad that I got the pieces I need." This is just a simple example of how a visual story about a real situation can provide the extra support a child needs to succeed. For more information, go to www.thegraycenter.org

I encourage families to use Social Stories™ whenever a tricky situation presents itself. I worked with a mother once who did an amazing job creating a "Going to the Park" Social Story™ for her son. He loved to play on several pieces of equipment but struggled with asking to change activities. The mom took pictures of everything that her son loved at the park and placed them in a small portable photo album. She then wrote a description statement about his favorites. She incorporated directive statements to instruct him on how to ask for each activity and how he could anticipate the transitions. Finally, she added a perspective statement, "Mommy is happy when I play nicely at the park" to a picture of her smiling to let her son know how she would feel.

Making Visual Supports

Remember this list of receptive and expressive visual supports is not anywhere close to exclusive. I see parents creating great supports every day. Time spent now making visual supports is time saved later as meltdowns and frustration on both sides are prevented.

Let's talk specifically about how you can make visual supports to assist your child. I have seen some very creative and beautiful systems, and I have seen some very simple systems. As long as you are choosing the most appropriate tools for your child, do not worry about aesthetics. In addition to the steps below, see *Making Visual Supports Work in the Home and Community: Strategies for Individuals with Autism and Asperger Syndrome* (Savner & Myles, 2000).

Lamination. I recommend that you make supports that last. After all, you will spend time making them, so let's build them to last. I always print my photographs and pictures on thick cardstock and then send them through a laminating machine. If you don't have access to a laminating machine, you can go to an office supply store or a teacher supply store and pay a small fee per square foot to laminate your pictures. (I have also been told that some stores sell small, personal laminators relatively inexpensively.) Some parents have told me that they simply wrap the pictures in clear packing tape to make them more durable. And one very creative parent taught me how to use laminating sheets with my own iron: Place your pictures between two pieces of laminate and put the laminate and pictures in a manila folder. Be sure no laminate is sticking out (or you will need a new iron!) and then use an iron to heat and seal the laminate.

Velcro. When it comes to velcro, I buy it in bulk when I can find it at a good price. Some families simply stick the velcro up all around the house. In the kitchen you will find it on the cupboards and on the refrigerator. In the bathroom there is velcro right on the mirror. And the entertainment center has strips of velcro to hold the movie photographs. After all, what better way is there to ensure consistency in a communication environment than when the environment is set up all the time.

Velcro does not stick to cold lamination.

Some children tend to perseverate on the velcro and need a different system. For them magnets may work. Buy long thin magnet strips at a craft store and cut them into smaller pieces. Place a magnet piece on the back of a picture. While the refrigerator is a natural place to put pictures with magnets, you can place cookie sheets of different shapes and sizes around the house for schedules, choice boards, and so on. Again, each system has to be individualized to the needs of the individual child. No one size fits all.

I also buy foam core board in bulk when I can find good prices and then I cut it into any shape I need; long strips for schedules, small squares for first/then boards, larger rectangles for choice boards, and so on. Another creative idea I learned from a parent was to find old carpet squares and use them instead of foam core board.

Organization. It is important to organize your pictures so you don't get overwhelmed and struggle to find pictures when you need them. Determine what will work best for your family. I usually get a large three-ring binder and fill it with thick, vinyl index dividers. I then place velcro or magnet strips row after row on the dividers and organize them by category (food, toys, people, etc.) to make it easy to find the picture I am looking for.

Several families I know have used baseball card holders to organize their pictures and inserted them into large three-ring binders. Organize them by category to make it easier to locate the picture you want. Or if it makes more sense to you, organize them alphabetically.

Another creative organizational tool is to get a set of small drawers used to hold screws and nails (you can buy at builder supply stores). You can label each drawer by category and then place the pictures inside. As always, there is no "one size fits all," just be sure the system is as functional for your family as possible so the time and effort spent creating the visual supports doesn't go to waste. Get creative and find the best system for you!

Final Thoughts

W I hope you have found lots of helpful ideas and strategies as you have read these pages. Certain ideas will stand out to you at different times when you read and re-read the book depending on where your child is in his or her development, so please don't think you have to create and implement everything right now. Pace yourself and prioritize. If you are working with a team, try to get support, guidance and help from your team members as you move forward.

Nevertheless, I do hope that you have found some specific strategies you can implement right now! Think about one or two things that stand out as "AHA!" moments (you know – the moment when the light bulb goes off) and start there. Just start so that the intervention can begin now. Remember, creating initiations and interactions with your child should be fun and motivating for everyone involved.

Have fun, enjoy your children and good luck.

References

Baker B., Landen S., & Kashima K. (1991). Effects of parent training on families of children with mental retardation: increased burden or generalized benefit? *American Journal of Mental Retardation, 96*, 127-136.

Bristol, M. (1993). Maternal depressive symptoms in autism: Response to psychoeducational intervention. *Rehabilitation Psychology, 38,* 3-9.

Brown, P., Sutterby, J., & Thornton, C. (2001). *Play is essential for brain development*. Children's Institute for Learning and Development. Retrieved from http://www.kiddysanook.com/article.php?id=6496&lang=en

Buron, K. D., Curtis, M. (2004). *Incredible 5-point scale: Assisting students with autism spectrum disorders in understanding social interactions and controlling their emotional responses*. Shawnee Mission, KS: Autism Asperger Publishing Company.

Cardon, T. (2004). *Let's talk emotions*. Shawnee Mission, KS: Autism Asperger Publishing Company.

Cardon, T. (2007). *Teach me to play [video]*. Shawnee Mission, KS: Autism Asperger Publishing Company.

Corbett, B. A. (2003). Video modeling: A window into the world of autism. *The Behavior Analyst Today, 4*(3).

Eckenrode, L., Fennell, P., & Hearsey, K. (2005). *Tasks galore*. Raleigh, NC: Tasks Galore.

First Signs, Inc. (2001). *First signs screening kit*. Merrimac, MA: Author.

Frost, L., & Bondy, A. (2002). *The picture exchange communication system training manual*. Cherry Hill, NJ: Pyramid Educational Products, Inc.

Gallagher, J. J. (1983). Families of handicapped children – Sources of stress and its amelioration. *Exceptional Children, 50*(10).

Gray, C. (2002). *Then new social story book*. Ft. Worth, TX: Future Horizons.

Greenspan, S., & Wieder, S. (1998). *The child with special needs*, Reading, MA: Addison-Wesley.

Harris, M. D., & Reichle, J. (2004). The impact of aided language stimulation on symbol comprehension and production in children with moderate cognitive disabilities. *American Journal of Speech-Language Pathology, 13*, 155-167.

Koegel, L., & Koegel R. (2006). *Pivotal response treatments for autism*. Baltimore: Paul H. Brookes Publishing Co.

Koegel, L., & LaZebnik, C. (2004). *Overcoming autism*. New York: Penguin Group.

Koegel, R. L., & Koegel, L .K. (1995). *Teaching children with autism: Strategies for initiating positive interactions and improving learning opportunities*. Baltimore: Paul H. Brookes Publishing Company.

Mayer Johnson. (2000). *Writing with symbols*. Solana Beach, CA: Author.

Melmed, R. (2003). *Autistic disorders screening kit*. Phoenix, AZ: SARRC.

Michel, D. E., & Jones, J. L. (1991). *Music for developing speech and language skills in children: A guide for parents and therapists*. St. Louis, MO: MMB Music, Inc.

Mirenda, P., & Locke, P. (1989). A comparison of symbol transparency in nonspeaking persons with intellectual disabilities. *Journal of Speech and Hearing Disorders, 54*, 131-140.

Prizant, B. (2002). The SCERTS model: Enhancing communication & socioemotional abilities of children with autism spectrum disorder. *Jenison Autism Journal, 14*(4).

Quill, K. (1996). Enhancing children's social-communicative interactions. In K. A. Quill, *Teaching children with autism* (pp. 163-189). Albany, Canada: Delmar.

Rocissano, L., & Yatchmink, Y. (1983). Language skills and interactive patterns in prematurely born toddlers. *Child Development, 54,* 1229-1241.

Savner, J., & Myles, B. (2000). *Making visual supports work in the home and community: Strategies for individuals with autism and Asperger Syndrome*. Shawnee Mission, KS: Autism Asperger Publishing Company.

Silver Lining Multimedia, Inc. (2000). *Picture this . . . professional edition*. Peterborough, NH: Author.

Sussman, F. (1999). *More than words*. Toronto, Canada: The Hanen Centre.

Tannock R., Girolametto, L. E., & Siegel, L. (1992). The interactive model of language intervention: Evaluation of its effectiveness for pre-school-aged children with developmental delay. *American Journal of Mental Retardation, 97*(2), 145-160.

TimeTimer, LLC. (1999). *Time-timer*. Cincinnati, OH: Author.

Watson, L. et al. (1989). *Teaching spontaneous communication to autistic and developmentally handicapped children*. Austin, TX: PRO-ED.

Wetherby, A., & Prizant, B. (1989). The expression of communicative intent: Assessment guidelines. *Seminars in Speech & Language, 10*(1), 77-91.

Wetherby, A., & Prizant, B. (1993). *Communication and Symbolic Behavior Scales – Normed Edition*. Baltimore: Paul H. Brookes Publishing Co.

Winner, M. (2002). *Thinking about you thinking about me*. San Jose, CA: Michelle Garcia Winner Publishing.

Wolfberg, P. (2005). *Peer play and the autism spectrum: The art of guiding children's socialization and imagination*. Shawnee Mission, KS: Autism Asperger Publishing Company.

Children's Books

Berenstain, S., & Berenstain, J. (1981). *The Berenstain Bears' Moving Day*. New York: Random House, Inc.

Berenstain, S., & Berenstain, J. (1982). *The Berenstain Bears Go to Camp*. New York: Random House, Inc.

Berenstain, S., & Berenstain, J. (1983). *The Berenstain Bears and the Messy Room*. New York: Random House, Inc.

Berenstain, S., & Berenstain, J. (1985). *The Berenstain Bears Learn About Strangers*. New York: Random House, Inc.

Berenstain, S., & Berenstain, J. (1986). *The Berenstain Bears and the Bad Habit*. New York: Random House, Inc.

Berenstain, S., & Berenstain, J. (1993). *The Berenstain Bears and the Bully*. New York: Random House, Inc.

Hefferan, R. (2003). *The Three Bears*. Toronto, Canada: Random House Inc.

Martin, B. (1995). *Brown Bear, Brown Bear*. Toronto, Canada: Henry Holt & Company.

Martin, B., & Archambault (1989). *Chicka Chicka Boom Boom*. New York: Simon and Schuster Books for Young Readers.

Mayer, M. (1983). *Just Grandma and Me*. Racine, WI: Western Publishing Company, Inc.

Mayer, M. (1983). *I Was So Mad*. Racine, WI: Western Publishing Company, Inc.

Mayer, M. (1988). *Just My Friend and Me*. Racine, WI: Western Publishing Company, Inc.

Mayer, M. (1991). *Little Critter at Scout Camp*. Racine, WI: Western Publishing Company, Inc.

McDonald, A. (1942). *Old McDonald Had a Farm*. Boston: Houghton Mifflin.

Ricci, C. (2004). *Dora's Book of Manners*. New York: Simon & Schuster Children's Publishing Division.

Santomero, A.C. (2000). *Blue Goes to School*. New York: Simon & Schuster Children's Publishing Division.

Secker, J. (2004). *Little Red Riding Hood*. Cambridge, MA: Barefoot Books.

Wilson, S. (2002). *Dora's Backpack*. New York: Simon & Schuster Children's Publishing Division.

APC

Autism Asperger Publishing Co.
P.O. Box 23173
Shawnee Mission, Kansas
66283-0173
www.asperger.net